VIET NAM

Travel with Marco Polo Insider Tips

INSIDER TIP
Your shortcut to a great experience

MARCO POLO
TOP HIGHLIGHTS

OLD HANOI ⭐
Traditional alleyways take you back to the days of the historic craft guilds.

➤ p. 42, Hanoi & the North

HA LONG BAY ⭐
Picture-perfect limestone islands surrounded by blue sea.
📷 *Tip: If it's foggy in winter, don't worry: it makes the scenery seem really mystical!*

➤ p. 55, Hanoi & the North

SA PA ⭐
The idyllic Sa Pa in the mountains of the northwest is a tourist magnet.
📷 *Tip: Ask people for permission before you take their photograph, as some believe that their spirit is "captured" when a snapshot is taken.*

➤ p. 60, Hanoi & the North

HUE CITADEL ⭐
The impressive residence of the Nguyen rulers recalls the days of the imperial dynasty.
📷 *Tip: Taking a selfie is a must – especially in a bright yellow royal costume.*

➤ p. 72, Hue & Central Vietnam

MY SON ⭐
It's definitely worth taking a trip to the temple ruins that were once the most important religious centre of the Cham people.

➤ p. 82, Hue & Central Vietnam

BOAT TOUR OF THE MEKONG DELTA ⭐ 8

Canals, temples and markets: an adventurous journey from My Tho on the waterways of the delta.

➤ p. 108, Ho Chi Minh City & the South

HOI AN ⭐ 6

A charming little city with magnificent Chinese shophouses, French colonial buildings and a Japanese covered bridge.
📷 *Tip: When the sun is going down, the surrounding area's rice fields are bathed in white light.*

➤ p. 83, Hue & Central Vietnam

CAO DAI TEMPLE ⭐ 9

The "holy seat" of Cao Dai supporters at Tay Ninh seems like a mix of cathedral, pagoda and mosque: you can watch the ceremonial prayer from the balustrade.

➤ p. 109, Ho Chi Minh City & the South

DA LAT ⭐

A summer resort developed by the French that is a magnet for lovers.
📷 *Tip: The blossom turns the whole of Da Lat pink under the cherry and apricot trees in spring.*

➤ p. 89, Hue & Central Vietnam

MUI NE ⭐ 10

A 16km-long beach, fishing boats and dunes that lend a Saharan feel: Mui Ne (photo) has stolen the top beach crown from Nha Trang.

➤ p. 119, Ho Chi Minh City & the South

CONTENTS

HANOI & THE NORTH

HUE & CENTRAL VIETNAM

HO CHI MINH CITY & THE SOUTH

CONTENTS

⏱ Plan your visit

£–£££ Price categories

(*) Premium-rate phone number

🍴 Eating & drinking

🛍 Shopping

🍸 Going out

🏖 Top beaches

(🗺 A2) Removable fold-out map
(🗺 a2) Additional map on the fold-out map
(0) Outside the area of the map

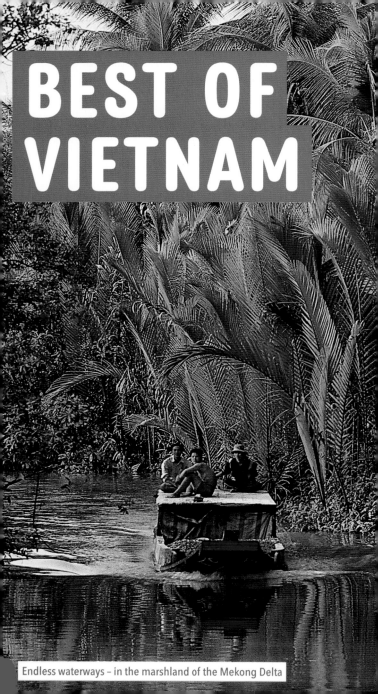

BEST OF
VIETNAM

Endless waterways – in the marshland of the Mekong Delta

BEST ☂

WHEN IT RAINS

ACTIVITIES TO BRIGHTEN YOUR DAY

ALL OF VIETNAM'S PEOPLE
The *Museum of Ethnology* in Hanoi provides a fascinating insight into the everyday lives of the many different peoples who make up Vietnam's population. You can even climb inside a traditional longhouse on stilts. (photo)
➤ p. 47, Hanoi & the North

SMELLS, CROWDS & NOISE
Shop and eat until midnight in the large *Dong Xuan market hall* in the old quarter of Hanoi. Fresh fish and sweets, lacquerware, T-shirts and … karaoke!
➤ p. 50, Hanoi & the Nor

SHIVA, GANESHA & MORE
The *Cham Museum* in Da Nang houses an amazing collection documenting the culture of the Hindu Cham people, who lived in central and south Vietnam for hundreds of years: sculptures and delicate reliefs from a lost empire.
➤ p. 80, Hue & Central Vietnam

AN ART DECO GEM
Journey back in time to imperial Vietnam. *Dinh 3* in Da Lat was the 26-room summer palace of Bao Dai, Vietnam's last emperor.
➤ p. 89, Hue & Central Vietnam

HO, HO, HO CHI MINH
At the *Ho Chi Minh Museum* you'll find original propaganda posters, and also meet school classes and local visitors finding out about the life and work of the father of their nation.
➤ p. 103, Ho Chi Minh City & the South

SHOP 'TIL YOU DROP
Treat yourself to a luxury shopping spree in Ho Chi Minh City. The *Vincom Center* is a shopping mall with many famous designers and fashion brands from all over the world represented. No fakes here, just expensive imports.
➤ p. 105, Ho Chi Minh City & the South

BEST ON A BUDGET

FOR SMALLER WALLETS

AN EARLY-MORNING WORKOUT WITH THE LOCALS

Early-bird athletes meet up every morning between 5am and 7am by *Lake Hoan Kiem* in Hanoi for aerobics, badminton or a jog around the lake. You don't have to be a tai chi expert to join in! (photo)

➤ p. 44, Hanoi & the North

QUEUING FOR HO CHI MINH

Tourists are invited to pay their respects to the country's revered father figure at Hanoi's *Ho Chi Minh Mausoleum*. After queuing alongside Vietnamese people from all over the country, you shuffle slowly past the glass sarcophagus.

➤ p. 46, Hanoi & the North

MILITARY PRECISION & TRADITION

At 9pm on the dot, with great military pomp, the Vietnamese flag is lowered on *Ba Dinh Square* in Hanoi. In today's turbo-capitalist society it's a nostalgic trip down memory lane, providing a glimpse of the "old" Vietnam, with its parade-ground discipline.

➤ p. 46, Hanoi & the North

HANOI TOUR WITH BUDDIES

A fun tour with Vietnamese young people: the students at *Hanoi e.Buddies* speak fluent English and are proud to show you their city and its traditions. Participants only pay for admissions, or snacks if you choose the culinary street-food tour.

➤ p. 51, Hanoi & the North

MULTICOLOURED TEMPLE

Visiting the main *Cao Dai Temple* in Tay Ninh is not free. But you can visit the *Cao Dai Temple* in Da Nang free of charge, and even take part in a service – you'll need to be as quiet as a mouse.

➤ p. 80, Hue & Central Vietnam

BEST WITH CHILDREN

FUN FOR YOUNG & OLD

PUPPET THEATRE ON WATER

Gongs and drums herald an exciting, funny show in which dragons spew fire and you can even hear rice grow! The puppets, sometimes over 50cm tall, perform on a stage consisting of a pool of water with a traditional backdrop. There are some very good performances, for example at the *Thang Long Water Puppet Theatre* in Hanoi.

➤ p. 51, Hanoi & the North

WIN POINTS FOR YOUR PANCAKES

Emperor Tu Duc once reigned in Hue and wanted 50 dishes served at every meal. You could aim for something similar if you really wanted to in Hue, but why not just go to a stall and try *banh ep*, a type of crêpe, served – for example – with cucumber or papaya? Children love this tasty street food!

➤ p. 75, Hue & Central Vietnam

ARTS AND CRAFTS

Crafting during your holidays? Why not? At *Truc Chi Garden* in Hue, you can learn how to magic up wonderful decorations from bamboo paper. Just start small – don't forget you'll want to take your artwork home with you!

➤ p. 76, Hue & Central Vietnam

FUN IN ANY WEATHER

The *Bach Ma National Park* offers lots to do, from trekking to abseiling. The 2km-long *Five Lakes Trail* is a real adventure: you need to climb on parts of it.

➤ p. 77, Hue & Central Vietnam

SANDCASTLES AND SWIMMING POOLS

Vietnam's beaches are legendary, with plenty of sand for sandcastles, But there's even more on offer for families: many hotel pools accept guests for the day for a small charge (usually around £4–£5).

BEST ⚑

CLASSIC EXPERIENCES

IN THE FOOTSTEPS OF CONFUCIUS
The *Van Mieu Temple of Literature* in Hanoi is the epitome of Confucian architecture. It was built almost 1,000 years ago in honour of the famed philosopher and political theorist.
➤ p. 45, Hanoi & The North

THE FUTURE FORETOLD
Look into the future at one of the hill tribe villages in *Sa Pa* or *Cao Bang*. A shaman offers rituals in front of a fire, with stones and bamboo used as a "telephone" to communicate with ancestors and spirits.
➤ p. 60 & p. 63, Hanoi & the North

SHAKE THE WOK!
A cookery course in Hoi An is a trip requisite. There is no better place to learn how to prepare spring rolls or a hot pot. For the best experience shopping for ingredients in the market and preparing them, try the *Brother's Café*.
➤ p. 86, Hue & Central Vietnam

A CYCLO ADVENTURE
A tourist on a three-wheeler *cyclo tour* might justifiably feel anxious as the driver cycles straight into the mêlée at a congested crossroads. But, somehow, a gap will miraculously appear.
➤ p. 98, Ho Chi Minh City & the South

DAVID VS GOLIATH
Crawl through Ho Chi Minh City's *Cu Chi Tunnels*, the underground complex used by the Vietcong in the Vietnam War. Afterwards, you will understand a little better how a small but determined David defeated the giant Goliath, with its napalm bombs. (photo)
➤ p. 108, Ho Chi Minh City & the South

ACTION ON THE MEKONG
Barges full of coconuts and rice, sampans with watchful eyes painted on the bow – the waterways of the Mekong Delta are busy around *Cai Rang Floating Market* near Can Tho.
➤ p. 113, Ho Chi Minh City & the South

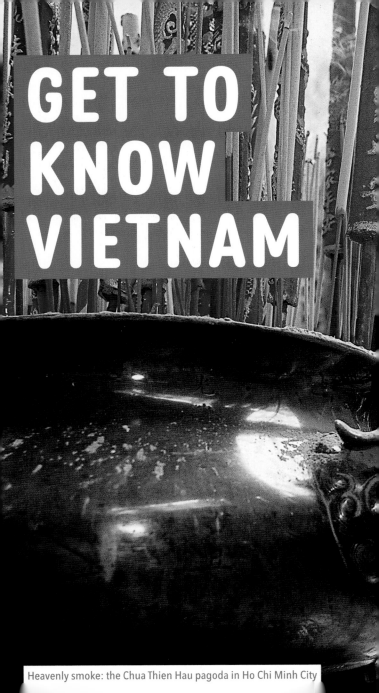

GET TO KNOW VIETNAM

Heavenly smoke: the Chua Thien Hau pagoda in Ho Chi Minh City

DISCOVER VIETNAM

A blaze of colour for the gods: the temple in the old imperial city of Hue

"Bonjour, madame." The old monk removes the woolly cap from his head and hands the foreign visitor a small card that reads, "Happy new year." The novice bows and presents a hairy, red rambutan fruit. Normally it's the visitors who offer gifts here, not the monks, but no one expects any offerings from tourists. Wind chimes tinkle in the breeze that blows through the hallowed halls of the temple. Breathe deep: at last you are somewhere away from the clatter of mopeds and the cacophony of hooting cars; a place to pause, a place for a dialogue with Buddha.

HISTORY AND NATURAL BEAUTY

Vietnam is a country moving swiftly into the future. Moss and a greenish patina shroud monuments thousands of years old, but on the streets of Ho Chi Minh

8th–4th century BCE
The Viet migrate from southern China

111 BCE–930 CE
North Vietnam is ruled by the Chinese. The Cham kingdom emerges from the 2nd century CE

938
Vietnam gains independence under General Ngo Quyen

1009
First stable dynasty under Ly Thai To. Thang Long (Hanoi) becomes the capital

1802
Hue becomes the home of the Nguyen emperor (until 1945)

1858
Start of French colonial rule

City and Hanoi, the modern world is everywhere. In fact, the cities often seemed poised between old and new. Beside broad, tamarind-shaded avenues, colourful Chinese temples sit alongside colonial mansions and weather-worn villas in shades of soft ochre. At the same time, the skyline rises higher with every blink of the eye. And mopeds are everywhere.

Away from the cities, visitors are charmed by the national parks, with their many species and treasures of the natural world, from the spectacular Ha Long Bay in the north to the Mekong Delta in the far south. In between, some 3,200km of coastline are dotted with islands, beaches and remote hideaways.

BEYOND THE VIETNAM WAR

Vietnam can look back on 4,000 years of history, but few other countries have suffered so painfully from wars and foreign invasion, and rule by the Chinese, the French, the Japanese and finally the Americans. The same nationalities are returning now, but this time they come in peace. Before the pandemic, around 18 million tourists visited the country and it was crowded everywhere. Tourist numbers fell during the global Covid-19 lockdowns of 2020–21, but numbers are recovering, with over 12 million visiting in 2023. Most of Vietnam's 97 million people moved on long ago from the country's most recent conflict, the Vietnam War. Half of all inhabitants are under 35 years old, so only know about it from history books. Sites like the Viet Cong tunnels and the Ho Chi Minh Museum give a valuable insight into this part of Vietnam's past, but the country has lots more to offer as well.

1954
Partition of Vietnam, military rule in the south

1964
Start of the Vietnam War, the communists win in 1975

2 July 1976
Foundation of Socialist Republic of Vietnam

2000
Bill Clinton is the first US president to visit Vietnam

2020–2022
The Covid-19 pandemic almost completely closes the country to tourists

2022
The world's longest glass bridge opened in northern Vietnam

HELLO MISTER!

The Vietnamese usually greet foreign visitors with a friendly, sometimes mischievous curiosity. Wherever there's a *tay*, a westerner, there's always something happening, something to laugh about. Vietnamese people do well from selling things to the *tay*, although some travellers regard their methods as intrusive. But if you don't react to their sales pitch, most traders quickly lose interest. Children try out their English and shout "I love you" or "Hello mister!". Respect for others, especially one's elders, is considered a virtue; it's a Confucian commandment, together with ancestor worship and hard work. Often up to three generations, which could number seven or eight people, live together in one room. Housing in Ho Chi Minh City has become unaffordable and the few available plots of land, houses or apartments change hands quickly.

WELCOME TO TURBO-CAPITALISM

Doi Moi, the economic reforms introduced by the Communist government in 1986, has transformed Vietnamese society. Profit is a new word in the Vietnamese vocabulary. The average annual income is estimated to be around £3,700 and the minimum monthly wage is £150. But in the last two decades, poverty has more than halved, though the rural–urban divide is still great. While the largest ethnic minority, the Chinese, dominate the business world, especially in the cities of southern Vietnam, most of the country's 54 ethnic groups live in the mountains and in the central highlands. Many of these ethnic groups are still in a transitional phase between a life revolving around ancient traditions, and modern life. Each group wears its own traditional clothes, celebrates its own festivals and follows its own customs.

AN ADVENTURE FOR ALL THE SENSES

Vietnam's scenic tropical beauty is enchanting, and the country has several natural UNESCO sites, from World Heritage Sites to biosphere reserves. Many visitors find themselves awestruck by Ha Long Bay, a UNESCO World Heritage Site with towering limestone cliffs, and the breathtakingly rugged "Vietnamese Alps" in the northwest, which can even get a covering of snow in cold winters. Near Phan Thiet, warm sand crunches underfoot on the beach at Mui Ne. Ho Chi Minh City has its dramatic tall skyline, and in the Mekong Delta the chugging engines of the long-tail boats provide an ever-present background beat. The whole Vietnam experience is topped off with a wide range of local Vietnamese regional dishes. Whether you are trying out rock climbing at Ha Long Bay, taking part in some slow-motion tai chi at dawn in Ho Chi Minh City, trying to see through the incense smoke at a pagoda, or feeling overwhelmed on your bike in the chaotic congestion of Hanoi, eventually your experiences will bring you closer to the Vietnamese, with their ubiquitous dragons and mysterious spirits.

AT A GLANCE

97,340,000
inhabitants

UK: 67,737,802

OVER 1,000
animal species have been discovered in the past 20 years, mostly insects

3,260km
of coastline

UK: 31,368km

332,800km^2
area

UK: 243,610km^2

**HIGHEST MOUNTAIN:
FAN SI PAN
(PHAN SI PANG)**
3,143m

Ben Nevis:
1,345m

POPULATION
54

ethnicities live in Vietnam, most of them in the mountainous regions

**LONGEST RIVER:
SONG HONG
(RED RIVER)**
510km

River Severn: 354km

THE MOST POPULAR TIME TO TRAVEL ...
... is for the TET Festival at the end of January/beginning of February, when thousands of Vietnamese people living abroad travel to Vietnam

MOST FAMOUS PERSON
Ho Chi Minh

HO CHI MINH CITY

Largest city with approx. 9 million inhabitants
London: 9.6 million

LONGEST AND DEEPEST CAVE IN THE WORLD
PHONG NHA-KE BANG

UNDERSTAND VIETNAM

SMART SPIRITS

Phuong has had bad headaches for days and doesn't know whether she should accept an office job as an assistant with a foreign company. She kneels with Ms Nguyen before the ancestral altar of her deceased grandfather, beneath his large black-and-white photo. As a medium, Ms Nguyen advises her, in the grandfather's name, to put a piece of red paper with Chinese characters under her pillow so the migraine will disappear. Phuong should also begin the new job the following new year.

In Vietnam, superstition stretches to shamans and feng shui consultants, miracle healers, faith healers and the four mythical animals (dragon, phoenix, tortoise and Qilin, a Chinese mythical and chimerical creature). Taoist superstitions – like unlucky days, lucky years or bad omens – are also part of daily reality.

Worshipping the ancestors maintains family ties after death. To ensure that deceased family members don't become restless spirits, they must be given incense and sacrifices like rice, tea, money, cigarettes and alcoholic drinks at the house altar. In the temples, paper money ("hell money"), paper houses, paper handbags and toy cars are burned.

SPECIAL "DELICACIES"

Welcome to the realm of aphrodisiacs. Here, too, superstition plays a role; Vietnamese men will eat a "virility enhancing" tiger penis and drink snake wine, or eat turtle eggs and bird's nest soup for a long life. Other "delicacies" include monkey brains, snake meat, civets and frogs. But don't worry, such dishes are expensive – locals would never offer them to an ignorant "long nose", as Westerners are called. In any case, they should be avoided in order to help protect endangered species.

WHERE SHIVA DANCES

The Hindu god Shiva also plays a role in Vietnam, or rather, he dances, if he is not travelling on his bull, Nandi. Those who want to explore the traces of an earlier culture in Vietnam should visit the Cham Museum in Da Nang. Between the sixth and 13th centuries, Champa was a powerful empire in southeast Asia, extending well into what is now Cambodia. Of the 250 temple sites that once belonged to the Cham civilisation, only 20 ruins now remain, one of which is My Son near Da Nang. The architecture and symbolism, such as the lingam, a (phallic) symbol for the Hindu god Shiva, clearly show that the early Cham were Hindus. Their successors, of whom about 100,000 still live in Vietnam, follow a moderate version of the Islamic faith, with its own festivals.

UNCLE HO

Presumably, the father of the nation would turn in his glass coffin if he was aware of all the fuss made of him today, with souvenir portraits and pop-art propaganda posters. It is well known that Vietnam's former president never wanted to be put on show in the way that he is at the Ho Chi Minh Mausoleum in Hanoi. In fact, he decreed in his will: "Divide my ashes into three parts and keep them in three ceramic urns that should be the symbol for the north, the centre and the south."

As a young revolutionary, Ho Chi Minh fought against French colonial rule, which dated from the 1880s to 1954. He founded the Communist Party of Vietnam in Hong Kong in 1930, and when the country was partitioned in 1954, he became president of the Democratic Republic of Vietnam, usually called North Vietnam. In July 1976, the country was reunited as the Socialist Republic of Vietnam, but it was not an event the still-revered "Uncle Ho" witnessed. He died on 2 September 1969 at the age of 79.

Beautiful ruins are all that is left of the Cham sanctuary, My Son

A DIVERSE NATURAL WORLD

More than 30 national parks and 130 nature reserves are waiting to be explored (hiking boots are essential).

INSIDER TIP
Singing gibbons

There's a real *Jungle Book* vibe in the parks, especially when the gibbons start their morning duets. The country's last rainforest areas are still a playground for several big cats, including the Indo-Chinese tiger, civet cat and clouded leopard, as well as elephants, black bears, jackals, skunks, mongoose, flying squirrels, red deer, crocodiles and pythons.

Although only around 12 per cent of Vietnam is still covered with tropical forests, those that remain are spectacular, and zoologists wax lyrical about them. Who would have thought that napalm-scorched and bombed Vietnam would be home to so many species? There are even several newly discovered species, including the antelope-like saola and the muntjac stag. The most enthralling national parks are *Cat Tien*, where some of the last wild elephants roam (you will also find them in *Yok Don*), and *Cuc Phuong*, with its primate protection project. The biosphere reserves that

Vietnam's daily bread: farmers gather their rice harvest

have the most species are *Cat Ba* and the remote *Phong Nha-Ke Bang*, with what is probably the world's biggest cave system.

FUN WITH ELEPHANTS?

Tourists and elephants in Asia – it's a tricky subject. Whether in Vietnam, Thailand or Cambodia, contact with domesticated elephants is usually a highly commercialised, lucrative business. Elephant camps are abundant, with a variety of offers, ranging from merely interacting with the animals, such as feeding and stroking them, to shows with "painting" elephants, tours with heavy seats, and *mahout* (trainer) courses lasting several days to gain an "elephant driver's licence". The line is continually blurred between sanctuary or retirement home for older elephants and business enterprises to entertain tourists. It is advisable to avoid all circus performances featuring elephants. In fact, a new trend has emerged, with tour operators beginning to cancel offers that include elephant shows. Get information from the relevant animal protection organisations before booking any elephant encounter. In *Yok Don National Park*, elephant rides have been banned since 2018.

LOCAL CRAFTS & FINE ART FAKES

So many souvenirs – and only one suitcase! But hey, wheelie suitcases are mega cheap in Vietnam ... The range of souvenirs and fine handicrafts is immense, and crafts have a long history here. It started with traditional new year pictures for the Tet festival – the black-and-white woodcuts known as *tranh tet* – and moved on to ceramics in the 11th century. Then came silk and lacquer painting in the 13th and 15th centuries, followed by sculpture and wood-carving. Today, hundreds of painters earn a living from copying western artworks. Replicas of works by Picasso or Rembrandt can be seen hanging on every street corner in Hanoi's *Old Quarter*. You can pick up a "Caravaggio" or a "Dalí" for £40 or less.

THE POWER OF RICE

Did you know that when Vietnamese people talk about food, they always talk about "eating rice", because rice is always there? For millennia, Vietnamese people have been grow-ing rice, and Vietnamese daily life would be unimaginable without it. Even legends and fairy tales talk about the national food. Today, Vietnam is one of the three top exporters of rice. In the Mekong Delta area alone there are three million people living as rice farmers: this is the area with the high-est yields because the Mekong water rises and falls regularly, perfectly watering the rice and ensuring up to three harvests per year.

TOLERANT CHAOS

The first visit to a temple in Vietnam can be a minor shock for the uninitiated: it's a confusing, loud mix of deities in a trumpet-sounding, incense-filled world. The pantheon of the gods is vast; the temples and pagodas are filled with gods and princes of hell alongside mythical heroes and generals, patron saints, demons and dragons. Rather than one Buddha, in Mahayana Buddhism at least three Buddhas ensure the path to enlightenment,

TRUE OR FALSE?

DOG IN THE PAN

Menus in Vietnam contain many exotic delights, such as roasted chicken claw, bat or turtle meat. Grasshoppers make a crispy snack to eat on the go. In the cold north, dog meat *(thit cho, thit cay)* is considered "warming" and "brings luck". But don't panic – no one is served this "speciality" without being aware of it. The delicacy is very precious to the locals and extremely expensive, so it would never creep into dishes without being advertised as such. So far, there are only rumours that serv-ing dog meat will be banned.

ENDLESS MOPED CHAOS

Vietnamese people drive every-where on their mopeds. Many of them don't even get off when shopping at the market or in shop-ping alleys: they simply stop and point at what they want as if they are glued to their moped seat. Old women at the markets with their produce or cooking stalls are the only ones who you see walking. However, pedestrian-only streets are on the rise. Alleys and night-time markets in the congested inner city are sometimes made into temporary pedestrian zones known as walking streets, with live bands and theatre, mostly at the weekend from 5pm to 11pm.

not forgetting the Bodhisattvas, the sentient beings, foremost among them being Quan Am. And while the Cham brought Hinduism to Vietnam, leaving traces of the faith behind, their descendants now practise Islam. Local religions and philosophies have also intermingled with Christianity: the most bizarre example is the Cao Dai cult, which was founded in 1926, and is a fusion of major religions supplemented by a pinch of the occult, the cult of celebrity and its own pope.

To make the confusion complete, there are many more influential guides to daily life and the afterlife. Some 2,500 years ago, Confucius was a philosophising lecturer who travelled across China popularising his ideas. For about a thousand years, Confucianism has also been the prevailing code of conduct within the family and society in Vietnam: young people are subordinate to their elders, women to men, subjects to their ruler. Since the 15th century, it has even influenced the structure of the state. Its five most important virtues are benevolence (or love), righteousness, propriety, wisdom and integrity. In everyday relationships, the oldest male is always the most respected person. So don't be surprised if the first question you are asked is your age!

There is no proof that Lao Tse actually existed, but as the founder of Taoism, he is responsible for everyday harmony in line with his esoteric, mystic teachings. Key symbols are the yin and yang (as female and male primary elements) and the Jade Emperor Ngoc Hoang as the universal ruler.

NO MORE WAR!

The Vietnamese prefer not to talk about the past. This mindset corresponds to a degree with the Taoist belief that if you constantly rake over tragic events, in the end you are inviting history to repeat itself. Between 1964 and 1975, the US waged an unprecedented war against the forces of the Viet Cong as part of a proxy war against global communism.

It is important to remember a few facts and figures from 11 years of the "American war": an estimated 3.5 million dead (soldiers and civilians, mostly Vietnamese), with 600,000 US and South Vietnamese soldiers fighting against 200,000 Viet Minh fighters and Viet Cong guerillas from communist North Vietnam. There were 7.5 million tons of bombs

Watter puppet theatre has been providing the finest entertainment for over a millennium

dropped from the air (with the same volume used on the ground), plus 80 million tons of the dangerous toxic chemical herbicide Agent Orange. The war created ten million refugees, and nobody knows the exact number of orphans, injured civilians, soldiers wounded in battle and stillbirths caused by toxins such as dioxin, used in Agent Orange, whose effects are still being felt today. There was also the devastation of huge swathes of land, villages and towns, and terrible massacres such as the one at My Lai. The financial cost to the US has been estimated at $176 billion.

Relations between the two former adversaries were only normalised in 1995, with a visit by Presdent Bill Clinton in 2000, 25 years after the Viet Cong victory.

LET THE PUPPETS DANCE

Things get wet, colourful, loud and fun at the water puppet theatre. Despite TV and social media, the tradition of *mua roi nuoc*, which dates back a thousand years, is still a cultural phenomenon.

This unique art form was probably developed as a form of entertainment by rice farmers. The puppets, made from fig tree wood, were modelled on villagers, animals, mythical creatures or spirits, and they are activated from below the water level with a bamboo stick. They weigh up to 15kg, so puppeteers need strength and skill, as they also stand in the water behind the curtain. It's still fun today, at least for the audience, thanks to stories from everyday life that are full of jokes and irony, as well the figures that whizz through the water.

EATING
SHOPPING
SPORT

A break amid red and gold: shops in Old Hanoi

EATING & DRINKING

Tu Duc, the fourth emperor of the Nguyen dynasty, who ruled the country from Hue between 1847 and 1883, had a passion for fine food. He wanted 50 dishes at every meal, prepared by 50 chefs and served by 50 waiters.

The kitchen staff did their utmost to comply with his wishes … and it's said that this is the reason why traditional Vietnamese cuisine boasts over 500 different dishes today.

WHITE RICE PLUS VARIETY

Those who like to eat well in Vietnam can use their chopsticks to tuck into a range of the most delicious dishes. And you can eat all day long, as traders man their sizzling food stands from early morning to late at night, selling everything from noodle soup and *banh mi* – the ubiquitous baguette snack – to BBQ feasts.

In restaurants, all the dishes you order — meat, fish and seafood, eggs, vegetables, salads and soups — are served at the same time, accompanied, of course by *com trang* (boiled rice). On the table will be plates with finely chopped vegetables or fresh herbs, such as basil, coriander, parsley, mint or lemongrass, which can be scattered over the dishes as required; lettuce leaves are also often included. Soups are eaten with a spoon and chopsticks, with the chopsticks used to fish the rice noodles or egg noodles out of the soup (*bun* or *pho*). Those who dare can sprinkle *nuoc mam*, the fish sauce made in factories in Phan Thiet and on the island of Phu Quoc, and used on every dish as a hearty condiment. The meal opens with the words *xin moi an* ("please tuck in"), whereupon everyone takes their chopsticks to fill their rice bowl and starts eating.

Tasty classic dishes: wafer-thin summer rolls *banh cuon* (l.) and *pho* soup (r.)

WHERE'S THE BEST FOOD?

Food choices range from fine dining in restaurants to small, roadside food stalls. In upmarket restaurants you will find western-style à la carte menus. In fact, many hotel restaurant chefs pander to the perceived preferences of western diners – hot flavours are toned down and a lot of fats are used. The many speciality restaurants in the major cities and tourist areas, however, are often excellent — proper gourmet eateries serving authentic dishes in a sophisticated ambience.

COLD NORTH, FIERY SOUTH

Because of the cooler climate in the north, the emphasis tends to be more on braised, fried and stir-fried dishes, and also on rice porridge. In the imperial heartlands around Hue, a number of restaurants geared towards tourism specialise in dishes once favoured by the imperial court, so the food is not just splendidly garnished and piquantly seasoned, but also appetisingly presented. If you are in Hue, then you are sure to see *banh khoai* on the menu: crispy pancakes with prawns, pork, bean sprouts and a sauce made from peanuts and sesame seeds.

In the south, more exotic, sometimes fiery, ingredients go into the pots and pans. The mixture is stirred briskly, sautéed briefly, grilled, and seasoned generously, sometimes with hot spices, for example in curries.

No trip to Vietnam is complete without trying the delicacies at one of the hot food stalls at the side of the road. Usually, they only serve soup or stew, for around £0.50 to £1.60. Restaurants outside large towns marked with *com pho* (rice soup) are usually also very good. English is a foreign language here, so make sure you write down the prices.

BALANCING ACT AT THE TABLE

Visitors to Vietnam are often advised to practise using chopsticks in advance if they're not familiar with them. You can always ask for a knife and fork, but it's much more fun to "do as the Romans do", and that means holding the two sticks delicately between thumb, forefinger and middle finger. Please note: the superstitious Vietnamese believe that chopsticks should never be left standing upright in your bowl: it symbolises death. It is impolite to poke around in the food, and it's better to just pick out individual bites. Pointing at people with chopsticks is also considered to be bad manners.

SWEET & SAVOURY

Some dishes mix sweet and savoury ingredients. *Banh bao* is a good example – small, sweet dumplings filled with meat and vegetables. And a Tet speciality for the Vietnamese New Year festival is *banh chung*, sticky rice cakes filled with beans and meat. You'll also find many different kinds of delicious desserts in Vietnam. *Banh deo* are sticky rice cakes soaked in sugar water and filled with fruit and sesame seeds. *Banh it nhan dao*, cakes made from mung bean starch, rice flour and sugar, are steamed in banana leaves. If you fancy candied fruit or vegetables – then order *mut*. Usually served with Vietnamese tea is a sugar-sweet, jelly-like mung bean cake, known as *banh dau xan*.

VITAMINS EN MASSE

The fruit selection is seemingly endless. You will find fruit at the markets, but also in temples as offerings, and each fruit has a particular symbolism: coconut, for example, stands for frugality; papaya for pleasure; cherimoya fulfils a wish; and plums are for longevity. In addition, dragon fruit gives strength; and the "eyes of the dragon" (*longans*, similar to *lychees*) are said to have a relaxing effect.

INSIDER TIP
The meaning of fruits

TO QUENCH THE THIRST

Quench your thirst with mineral water *(nuoc soi)* or all kinds of colas and soft drinks. But do not overlook drinks such as the ubiquitous green tea *(che)*, fresh coconut milk (*nuoc dua*) or tasty tropical fruit juices *(sinh to)*. Rice wine may not be to everyone's taste, but few people could dislike the beer – either as a *bia hoi* (draft beer) or as Castel, Huda (from Hue), Saigon Export, Bia Hanoi, Salida or 333 (pronounced *ba ba ba*). Costing just £0.40 to £0.85 a glass, it is very affordable; but in a *bia hoi* corner bar, where you sit on a stool in the open air, you can buy beer for even less.

Vietnamese coffee is very good and very strong. When coffee is served, a special metal filter and ground coffee is placed on top of the cup. Boiling water is then poured on to the coffee, which drains slowly through into the cup containing a generous quantity of condensed milk.

TODAY'S SPECIALS

Starters

CHA GIO
Crispy spring rolls filled with prawns, pork, mushrooms, carrots and cellophane noodles, also known as *nem ran*

BANH CUON
Wafer-thin crêpes made from steamed rice flour, filled with minced meat, onions and herbs, also known as summer rolls

Main meals

BUN CHA
Delicious, marinated pork patties cooked on the charcoal grill, served with long rice noodles

CHA CA
Tasty marinated fillets of fish, cooked on the BBQ and then deep-fried

GA KHO GUNG
Caramelised chicken with ginger, sugar and pepper

HOT POT
A kind of Vietnamese fondue with fish, seafood, beef, vegetables and glass noodles, cooked in a simmering stock at the table

Desserts

BANH CHUOI
Pancakes made from small sweet bananas

BANH DEO
Also called "mooncakes": small golden cakes with a filling made of lotus nuts and mung beans

Snacks

BANH MI
The Vietnamese sandwich is a baguette. Tip: try one with pork and herbs

BUN THANG
A substantial soup of rice noodles, chicken, pork sausage and omelette strips

MIEN GA
Chicken soup with cellophane noodles, mushrooms and shallots

CANH CHUA
Sweet and sour fish soup with tamarind, soybean sprouts and coriander

PHO
The classic dish: rice noodle soup from the north, with beef, chicken or prawns

SHOPPING

GOOD HATS

Good-quality traditional conical hats have thin scraps of paper between the straws. The finest hats come from the Hue region. In the hatters' village of Phu Cam (also Phuoc Vinh) on the south bank of the An Cuu river, the women produce semi-translucent hats made from palm leaves, which they decorate with silk thread, images of the landscape or lines of poetry (also available in the *Dong Ba Market* in Hue).

BUY RUBBISH

In the Mekong Delta region alone, 4,000 tonnes of rubbish are created every day. A World Wildlife Fund project wants to provide support for waste sorting and making old from new, so Vietnamese people can make money from their waste, hopefully in a sustainable fashion. However, making use of waste is not new in Vietnam. The Vietnamese have been creating interesting recycled products, such as printed wallets made from cement bags and flip flops, for some time. The waste available ranges from Jeep tyres left behind by the US soldiers in the Vietnam War to plastic waste from the beach and tattered fabric rice sacks.

EMBROIDERY, PAINTING, CARVING

Silk, hand-painted or printed cotton fabrics, embroidery, copper and silver *objets d'art*, porcelain, jewellery, statues, wood carvings, miniatures, leather goods, carpets and beautiful furniture with inlays are all available at reasonable prices. These days, gigantic out-of-town halls filled with handicrafts welcome customers. One example is the *Hong Ngoc Humanity Center (on the N18 between Hanoi and Ha Long City | Sao Do | Hai Duong)*. People go there in search of the ultimate souvenir.

Treat yourself to soemthing colourful: funny masks (l.) and shiny siks (r.)

How about a statue of Ho Chi Minh in white marble for your terrace at home? At the foot of the Marble Mountains, in the village of Quang Nam, master sculptors are kept hard at work — you can hear the hammering from up in the mountains.

FINE SILK CLOTHES

In the silk shops, such as those in "Tailor Town", Hoi An, you can have clothes made for you at very affordable prices. If you would like an *ao dai*, the national dress for Vietnamese women, you can get one from around £25, but you will pay more for real silk.

PICTURES FROM COLOURFUL SAND

Sand paintings *(tranh cat)* make for decorative souvenirs. In Nha Trang, the *Hong Chau Sa family* sell works of art depicting everything from landscapes to Santa Claus. The colourful sand comes from Phan Thiet, where you will also find *Phi Long Sandpainting (113 Van Hanh | FB: sandartvietnam).* Want your portrait done in sand? The best-known artists do portraits on request, and you'll find images of the likes of Marilyn Monroe or the Pope, for example in Ho Chi Minh City at *Kim Sa, Sand Painting My Art (tranhcatmyart.com).*

INSIDER TIP Captured in sand

GLAMOROUS SHIFT WORK

The resin of the *son* tree is collected and made into brown or black lacquer, which is used to decorate accessories and homewares – anything from a tea set to lounge suites – as lacquerware. For a more expensive piece in a specialist store, ask how many layers were applied. The more layers, the more valuable the item. Ten is the minimum number; the maximum could be 200.

SPORT & ACTIVITIES

The range of activity holidays in Vietnam is gradually widening, but some sports and activities, such as caving, are still new here.

Beware: safety standards at some companies are still rudimentary. As a rule, the cheaper the tour or activity, the more inexperienced the guides are likely to be.

CAVING

Superlatives are not enough: this is the most beautiful, deepest, exciting to explore and species-diverse – as well as possibly the largest – cave in the world! Keen cavers love discovering the vast chambers in the *Phong Nha Cave (Son Trach, 55km northwest of Dong Hoi, Central Vietnam | phong nhakebang.vn)*. Caving here is organised by *Phong Nha Farmstay (Cu Nam, Dong Hoi | tel. 094 4 75 98 64 | phong-nhacave.com | tour approx. £25–£250, book well in advance)*. You can also visit the cave by boat *(admission from approx. £6 per person, approx. £20 per person for a group, for some tours you also have to pay for the boat)*. A tried-and-tested tour operator is *Footprint Travel (18A Ngo Tat To, Van Mieu | Hanoi | tel. 024 39 33 28 44 | footprint.vn)*.

The almost 9km-long *Hang Son Doong Cave (sondoongcave.org)* is also absolutely spectacular. Its interior vaults are up to 200m high – higher than many cathedrals – and those who are daring enough can camp overnight next to an underground lake *(son doongcave.org)*. Those who like a warm shower will not want to go on the week-long, very adventurous treks ($3,000 | only 200 visitors per year climbing experience essential, long waiting list | oxalis.com.vn).

INSIDER TIP Cathedral-like cave

Marvel at the view as you paddle on a kayaking tour of Ha Long Bay

CYCLING

For longer routes, cyclists should bring their own bike and also a good selection of spare parts. Good bikes (rental costs approx. £0.80 to £1.60 per day) are rare in Vietnam, as are bike shops with a proper supply of spare parts.

Favourite cycling areas include the flat Mekong Delta, as well as trips around the cities of Hoi An and Hue, and the Tam Coc region. Avoid the N1 (heavy traffic, dangerous sections). For some routes, you can switch to lovely coastal roads (such as the Coastal Highway 702 north of Phan Rang up to Nha Trang, which runs for approximately 100km) or the new Ho Chi Minh Highway through fantastic countryside (although it is sometimes quite mountainous and sparsely populated, with limited accommodation available). *Vietnam Tours (tel. 021 43 25 00 34 | vietnam-tours.de);* *World Insight (tel. 022 0 39 25 57 00 | world-insight.de).*

DIVING

Nha Trang, Phu Quoc, the coast off Hoi An and the Con Dao archipelago are the best sites in Vietnam for diving. Nha Trang and Phu Quoc boast a number of diving schools. Visibility underwater here is on average 10–15m, and up to 30m during the dry season. Among around 25 dive sites in the country, the best conditions are to be found around Con Dao: the "Fish Highway" enjoys up to 45m of visibility. In addition to relatively well-preserved hard and soft corals, there are also tropical fish, as well as sand sharks and oceanic whitetip sharks. Two dives (one tank each) cost from approx. £70. *Rainbow Divers (divevietnam.com).*

GOLF

Golf is the latest craze in the "new Vietnam". There are several golf courses suitable for both professional and amateur players, such as the ones near Hanoi and Ho Chi Minh City, and in Phan Thiet and Da Lat. The *BRG Kings Island (brgkingsislandgolf.vn)* can be found in the north, in Son Tay near Hanoi.

HIKING

The best areas for hiking are the *Bach Ma National Park*, the hilly area around Sa Pa, the *Ba Be National Park* and the highlands near Da Lat, such as *Mount Lang Biang*. You should bring your own equipment, including boots, walking poles, rucksack, water bottles and energy bars. However, you can also buy high-quality trekking equipment in Ho Chi Minh City, Hanoi and Sa Pa. Recommended tour operator: *Phat Tire Ventures (109 Nguyen Van Troi, Da Lat | tel. 092 7 79 89 37 | ptv-vietnam.com).*

KAYAKING TOURS

By far the best sea-kayak tour available is through Ha Long Bay. You can choose from tours of between one and six days in length, all with an English-speaking guide. Some 6–8km are covered per day, depending on the group's fitness level and the number of caves being visited. Multi-day tours

Tai Chi helps improve your balance, so get up early and join in!

involve overnight stops in tents; luxury offers include accommodation on a boat. Two-day tours including meals cost from around £170 per person. Book through reputable tour operator *Footprint Vietnam (footprint. vn)* or with *Inserimex Travel (inserimextravel.com.vn)*.

ROCK CLIMBING

Ha Long Bay and *Lan Ha Bay* near Cat Ba are perfect destinations for rock climbers. The views are terrific, the challenges great. But if you want to climb independently, you must bring your own equipment. You also need the experience of guides, who know the tides, as access to many of the

caves inside the giant limestone rocks is only possible when the water is at a certain level. Information and tours (with trained climbers and equipment): *Cat Ba Asia Outdoors (tel. 083 4 55 52 08 | FB: Catba outdooradventures)*.

SURFING & SAILING

One excellent windsurfing beach is *Mui Ne* near Phan Thiet *(windsurfvietnam.com)*. Competitions such as the *Starboard Vietnam Fun Cup* are staged here. For more information, contact *Jibe's Club (Mui Ne | jibes beachclub.com/water-sport-center)*. There's windsurfing at the *Full Moon Beach Resort (lessons approx. £42/hr | km 13.5, Ham Tien | tel. 025 23 84 70 08 | fullmoonbeach.com.vn)*. The *Mia Resort (24 Nguyen Dinh Chieu, Ham Tien | tel. 025 23 84 74 40 | miamuine.com)* offers surfing and kitesurfing. Vietnam's sailing scene likes to gather in the coastal resorts of *Nha Trang* and *Mui Ne/Phan Tiet*.

TAI CHI

If you are interested in the Chinese martial art of tai chi (or *thai cuc quyen* in Vietnamese), you will have to get up early. Classes take place in Ho Chi Minh City from Tuesday to Saturday at 5.30–7am and 7–8.30am in *Le Van Tam Park (Hai Ba Trung/corner Dien Bien Phu)* for a small contribution. There are also classes in *Van Hoa Park*, in *Tao Dam Cultural Park (approx. 8–9am)* and in the *"23/9" Park (Pham Ngu Lao)*. In Hanoi, classes are held by *Lake Hoan Kiem* and in the *Botanical Garden*.

REGIONAL OVERVIEW

CHINA

Sa Pa
Thái Nguyên

HANOI

MYANMAR

Mekong

HANOI & THE NORTH p. 38

LAOS

Thanh Hóa
Vinh

THAILAND

Lively cities, enticing beaches, and drifting along on the Mekong

HO CHI MINH CITY & THE SOUTH p. 94

Gulf of Thailand

Cần Thơ'

Witness changing times in the land of the hill tribes

Gulf of
Tonkin

CHINA

HUE & CENTRAL VIETNAM p. 68

Huê

Đà Nang

Hội An

On the trail of emperors and Cham culture

S o u t h

C h i n a

S e a

CAMBODIA

Quy Nhơn

Đa Lat

Nha Trang

Chi
nh City

Múi Né

200 km
124.28 mi

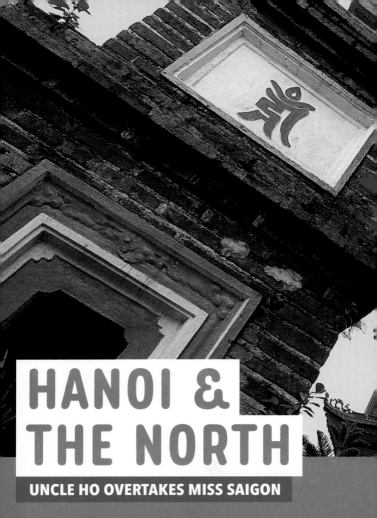

HANOI &
THE NORTH

UNCLE HO OVERTAKES MISS SAIGON

It's a bit like a competition: bigger, higher, quicker. For a long time, Hanoi, once a centre of communism in the country, was regarded as the quieter of Vietnam's two major cities, with its almost sleepy charm and bright colonial buildings.

There is no holding Hanoi back now, with its construction boom and skyscrapers. But the enchanting parks, idyllic lakes and the remaining quiet corners of the city more than make up for that. The north is also full of natural wonders: about three hours away from

Close to the skies: a pagoda in Hanoi

Hanoi by car, the white limestone rocks of Ha Long Bay, overgrown with jungle greenery, jut out of the water – definitely one of Vietnam's top tourist hotspots. The mountain town of Sa Pa is developing rapidly, and the hill tribes in the vicinity are on a journey into modern life.

To experience the beauty and authenticity of the region away from the hubbub of the busier mountain areas – with a photo-worthy rice terrace as your backdrop – visit Ba Be National Park. This evergreen tropical rainforest is well worth a trip and is still a fairly well-kept secret.

HANOI & THE NORTH

16 Dong Van

Meo Vac **17**

Yên Minh

马关县
Maguan

● **Ha Giang**
p. 66

Vị Xuyên   Yên Phú

Mường Khương

河口县
Hekou

12 Bac Ha

Lào Cai

~100km, 2½ hrs~

2

● **Sa Pa** ★
p. 60

Phố Lu

Việt Quang

Tân Uyên

Phố Ràng

Khánh Yên

VIỆT NAM

Tân Yên

Than Uyên

Mậu A

Tuyên Quang

Mù Cang Chải

Ngòi Tha

11 Mu Cang Chai

Liễn Sơn

Yên Bái

2

Trấn Phú

Phong Châu

Sơn La

Yên Lập

Việt Trì

6

Phù Yên

Thanh Sơn

Duong Lam **7**

Sông Mã

Yên Châu

Đà Bắc   Kỳ Sơn

ຊຽງຄໍ
Muang Xiangkho

6 Bach Long Glass Bridge ★
(White Dragon)

Hoa Binh **5**

ຊ ບເບ່າ
Sốp Bao

6

Mai Châu

Mường Khến

ປະເທດລາວ
LAOS

Quan Hóa

MARCO POLO HIGHLIGHTS

★ **OLD HANOI**
Picturesque artisans' houses and bustling street markets ➤ p. 42

★ **LAKE HOAN KIEM**
This idyllic city lake in Hanoi is not just a lovers' rendezvous ➤ p. 44

★ **VAN MIEU**
Confucian simplicity, but with impressive proportions: the Temple of Literature in Hanoi ➤ p. 45

★ **HA LONG BAY ON LAND**
A fairy-tale landscape near Ninh Binh – with rocks as far as the eye can see ➤ p. 52

★ **HUONG TICH SON**
A magnificent karst landscape and the Perfume Pagoda ➤ p. 53

★ **BACH LONG GLASS BRIDGE (WHITE DRAGON)**
Get an adrenaline rush on the spectacular glass bridge set among rugged mountains ➤ p. 54

★ **HA LONG BAY**
Simply outstanding – limestone pinnacles emerging from the sea ➤ p. 55

★ **SA PA**
Get close to the colourfully dressed hill tribes in the rugged mountains of the northwest ➤ p. 60

HANOI

(▢ E3) **In Hanoi (pop. approx. 4.8 million), you encounter all the superlatives: one of Asia's most beautiful and oldest cities presents a virtual *Who's Who* of Vietnamese history.**

You'll come across heroes from Confucius to Ho Chi Minh, alongside modern signifiers of today's fast-paced turbo-capitalism – including the property boom and traffic chaos. Since 2021, you can dive into the quiet and relaxing underground: travelling on the first underground train system in Vietnam is a bargain *(Line 2 Cat Linh in the southwest of the city | day ticket approx. £1.10).*

The city was founded in 1010. However, it was not named *Ha Noi*, or the "city on the bend of the river", until the days of Emperor Minh Mang (1820–41). Spacious parks and around 600 temples, pagodas and magnificent buildings from the European colonial era shape the face of the city. And after the economic boom reached the north of Vietnam, this vast metropolis got moving. Mopeds roar through the streets, the noise of construction work is ever-present, housing and office blocks are springing up everywhere, and today, as in the past, the wealthy stay and host events in its luxury hotels.

SIGHTSEEING

OLD HANOI ★

No visitor could possibly ignore Hanoi's Old Quarter. The artisans' district, which was first settled in the 11th century, when Emperor Ly Thai To moved the capital here, is a fascinating sight. The "36 streets" from that time have survived the centuries. Each is named after the goods that were once sold there: *Hang Ca* is Fish Lane, *Hang Bo* Basket Street, *Hang Buom* Sailmakers' Alley, *Hang Non* for hatters and *Hang Hom* for carpenters who made coffins. Unfortunately, the brick houses from the 19th century are threatened by the construction boom.

From 3pm during the week – reaching fever pitch during the 5pm to 9pm rush hour – two-wheeled chaos reigns, accompanied by overwhelming noise and a strong smell of fuel. It's sometimes almost impossible to move, either because the narrow pavements are crammed with parked mopeds, or

---

WHERE TO START?

Start your tour of the city with a walk round **Lake Hoan Kiem** *(▢ k3–4)*, from the French (Hotel) Quarter at the southern end of the lake, past the "gymnasts" (you'll find them in the early morning and evening), and the Jade Mountain Temple (Den Ngoc Son), and then on into the heart of the Old Quarter. If you're a long way from the starting point, take the *Electric Car Tour*, for example, from the Water Puppet Theatre or Dong Xuan market. Or you can take a moped taxi or bus there, numbers 1, 3, 7 or 14.

HANOI

The Summit Lounge
Hanoi Rock City
Foodshop 45
Hồ Tây
Hồ Trúc Bạch
Ngõ 71 Tân Ấp
Nghĩa Dũng
Yên Phụ
Châu Long
Cửa Bắc
Hàng Bún
Hàng Than
An Xá
Phúc Xá
Sông Hồng
Cầu Long Biên
Den Tran Vu
Quán Thánh
Phan Đình Phùng
Museum of Ethnology
Ho Chí Minh House
Lý Nam Đế
Dong Xuan Market
Tri Phương
Ho Chi Minh Mausoleum
Chua Mot Cot
Citadel
Hoàng Diệu
Nguyễn
Điện Biên Phủ
Hàng Cót
Hanoi Gallery
Old Hanoi ★
Café Bar Nola
Tube House on Ma May Street
Mekong Quilts
Highway 4
Lê Hồng Phong
Top of Hanoi
Trần Phú
Nguyễn Thái Học
Bun Cha Dac Kim
Trần Phú
Hàng Bông
Den Ngoc Son
Thang Long Water Puppet Theatre
Van Mieu ★
Craft Link & Hoa Sen Gallery
Lotus Water Puppet Theatre
Hanoi Social Club
Lake Hoan Kiem ★
Lê Lai
Tôn Đức Thắng
Hai Bà Trưng
Tràng Thi
Chua Quan Su
Bar & Jazz Club Minh's
Le Bon Steak House
Opera House
iBiero
Craft Beer Station
Quang Trung
Bà Triệu
Hàng Bài
Cong Caphe (Hoang Cau)
Lê Duẩn
Yết Kiêu
Trần Bình Trọng
Nguyễn Du
Cong Caphe (Thai Ha)
500 m
547 yd
Khâm Thiên

because the congested streets are overflowing with hundreds of mopeds revving and hooting. If there's room, riders simply drive on the pavement – at breakneck speed. The best solution is to just wait it out with tea in one of the chic cafés or a *bia hoi* beer in an air-conditioned bar. Or, you can come at weekends when the small streets around the Dong Xuan are transformed from Friday to Sunday afternoon into relaxing pedestrian zones. 📖 *j–k 2–3*

TUBE HOUSE ON MA MAY STREET ⚑

Slip on felt slippers to shuffle along in, and be amazed: this wooden house dating from the 19th century is in fine shape. The *Ngoi Nha Di San Heritage House* was restored and opened to visitors as a typical example of this kind of very narrow building, known as a "tube house", which can be 60–80m deep, in other words, like a tube. This one is only 28m deep, but it is full of antiques. The finely carved swing doors and the brick carvings, which promise a long life, are well pre-served. And don't miss the beautiful antique bed with mother-of-pearl decorations on the top floor. *Daily 8am–5pm | admission approx. £0.50 | 87 Ma May |* ⏱ *30 mins | ▥ k3*

> **INSIDER TIP**
> A magnificent bed

LAKE HOAN KIEM ★

Imagine you are strolling around the lake. It's still early and the water is covered in mist. Suddenly, a gleaming golden turtle appears; it carries a glinting sword. Unlikely? If you look at the water for long enough, perhaps you can believe it, as the Vietnamese do. Legend has it that in the 15th century, the heroic Le Loi took a magical sword from a golden turtle in the "Lake of the Returned Sword", and used it to drive the Chinese out of Vietnam. Having successfully achieved that, the magic sword was seized from Le Loi's sheath and restored to the turtle in the lake. As a gesture of gratitude, the *Thap Rua*, or Turtle Tower, was built on an island in the middle of the lake. Incidentally, for decades a 200kg

Listen to Confucian teachings at the Van Mieu literature temple

giant softshell turtle really lived in the lake – it died at a grand age in 2016 and can be seen in a glass box in the *Den Ngoc Son Temple*.

🐢 Every morning between 5am and 7am, the lakeside resembles a fitness centre as joggers, gymnasts, tai chi and aerobic enthusiasts meet to get their daily fix of exercise. It costs nothing to join in. In the evenings, activities are more geared towards hip hop and breakdance. 🗺 *k3–4*

DEN NGOC SON

The fire-engine red "Jade Mountain Temple" really catches the eye at night, when it is dazzlingly lit. You can reach it by going across the Huc Bridge, the red "Bridge of the Rising Sun", to the island in Hoan Kiem Lake. The temple is dedicated to three individuals: General Tran Hung Dao, who defeated the Mongols during the 13th century; the scholar Van Xuong; and La Tho, the patron saint of physicians. The Den Ngoc Son Temple is also home to the preserved Cu Rua turtle, which lived to over 100 years old in the Hoan Kiem Lake until its death in 2016. It is said to be the last descendant of the turtle deity from Vietnamese mythology, Kim Qui, known as the "Golden Turtle" and guard of the magical "returned sword". *Daily summer 7am–6pm, winter 7.30am–5.30pm | admission approx. £1.30 | ⏱ 45 mins (depending on crowds) | 🗺 k3*

CHUA QUAN SU

The "Ambassadors' Pagoda" is always a hive of activity, but this isn't surprising as it's the city's Buddhist centre.

During the 15th century the building was used as a hostel for Buddhist emissaries from other countries. *Daily approx. 6am–9pm | 73 Quan Su | ⏱ 30 mins | 🗺 j4*

VAN MIEU ★ 🚩

You might not get this close to Confucius ever again: you need to step through four gates to see the altar dedicated to the wise man. Ly Thanh Tong, the third ruler of the Ly Dynasty, had the "Temple of Literature" built in 1070 in honour of Confucius. Only six years later, Vietnam's first university was founded in an adjoining property: Quoc Tu Giam, the institute for "Sons of the State".

The route to the master begins at Quoc Tu Giam street. First, you pass through the *Van Mieu Portal* in the forecourt. The paved path leads up to the first gate, *Dai Trung*, the "Gate of the Great Middle", and then to the *Khue Van Cac*, the "Pleiades Gate", leading into a pavilion dating from 1805. Literary debates and poetry readings were held here. In the courtyard at the rear, stone turtles, symbols of wisdom, are clustered around the *Thien Quang Tinh*, the "Well of Heavenly Clarity". They bear 82 stone stelae on their backs, dating from between 1442 and 1779, inscribed with the names of the Confucian Academy's successful graduates.

Pass through the *Dai Thanh Gate* ("Gate of Great Success") and enter the fourth, most important courtyard in the temple buildings and its ceremonial heart, with a hall honouring Confucius's 72 wisest disciples and the *Thuong Dien* building, with an altar dedicated to Confucius.

Behind it is the fifth and final courtyard, *Thai Hoc*, where you will find a museum and, on the second floor, altars with statues of the kings Ly Nhan Tong, Ly Thanh Tong and Le Thanh Tong. *Daily 7.30am–5.30pm | admission approx. £0.85 | ⏱ 30 mins–1 hr | ▥ h4*

CITADEL

For over 50 years the Citadel was closed off as a military zone, but the first rebuilt sections are now open to the public. Completed between 1802 and 1812, it was built on the orders of Emperor Gia Long to a design drawn up by French military architects. The French captured the fortress in 1872 and destroyed most of it. Visitors can enter the inner Citadel via the *Doan Mon* central gate *(19c Hoang Dieu)* on the western side, at the level of the *Ho Chi Minh Mausoleum*. *Daily 8am–5pm | admission approx. £1 | hoangthanhthanglong.vn/en | ⏱ 30 mins–1 hr | ▥ h–j 2–3*

HO CHI MINH MAUSOLEUM 🐗

Built between 1973 and 1975, the massive blocks of red, black and grey marble create an awe-inspiring venue for the last resting place of Ho Chi Minh. In silence and usually after waiting in a long queue, visitors parade past the glass coffin containing the mortal remains of the country's great revolutionary. It was here, on 🐗 *Ba Dinh Square*, in front of where the mausoleum now stands, that Ho Chi Minh declared Vietnam's independence on 2 September 1945. With full military pomp, a flag is hoisted every morning at 6am and then lowered again at 9pm. No admission in shorts, mini-skirts or tank tops, and cameras must be handed in before entry. *April–early Sept Tue–Thu 7.30–10.30am, Sat, Sun 7.30–11am, early Dec–Mar Tue–Thu 8–11am, Sat, Sun 8–11.30am, early Sept–early Dec generally closed | admission free | ⏱ 1 hr (depending on length of queue) | ▥ g2*

CHUA MOT COT

There's a charming legend behind the "One Pillar Pagoda". One night the goddess Quan Am appeared before the ageing and childless emperor Ly Thai To, and presented him with a baby boy. There was now a male heir in the royal family and so, out of gratitude to the goddess, Ly Thai To built a stone pillar in the form of a lotus flower as a memorial shrine. In 1954 the column was destroyed by the French, but a concrete replica was built as a replacement. It's not an architectural masterpiece, but the unusual construction attracts a lot of visitors. The most atmospheric photos can be taken early in the morning or in the early evening in the soft light. Quan Am is still revered as a symbol of fertility. *Daily sunrise to sunset | Chua Mot Cot street, south of the Ho Chi Minh Mausoleum | ⏱ 20 mins | ▥ g2*

HO CHI MINH HOUSE

Long queues regularly form outside the wooden house where Ho Chi Minh lived from 1958 until his death in

In the Ho Chi Minh House, you can see how the leader lived

1969. Because of this, any insights into the life of "Bac Ho" (Uncle Ho) from the rather sparse office, the no less spartan bedroom and the pond, where he often sat and mused, can be time limited. *Daily 8–11am, 1.30–4pm | admission approx. £1.30 | Ba Dinh Square, next to the Presidential Palace (in the park) | ⏱ 30 mins | ▥ g2*

MUSEUM OF ETHNOLOGY

Fifty-four ethnic peoples in one place – and you only need a morning or afternoon to get to know them all! This museum, with indoor and outdoor exhibits, is fun, whether you listen to traditional music, watch the water puppets with their wet and cheerful show, or scale an Ede tribal longhouse in the giant open-air section.

The original life-size models of the tribespeople are outside, but the traditional costumes, musical instruments and handicrafts displayed inside reflect the great variety of ethnic peoples in Vietnam. Exhibits include an original lunar calendar that folds out like a fan, consisting of 12 bamboo bars with optimal dates for harvest, building houses, weddings or burials, and is said to bring luck. Because of the many figures and puppets, this museum will also fascinate kids. *Tue–Sun 8.30am–5.30pm | admission approx. £1.30 | Nguyen Van Huyen, northern outskirts on the route to the airport (journey time from city centre 25 minutes) | vme.org.vn | ⏱ 2–3 hrs | ▥ 0*

INSIDER TIP
Lucky calendar

DEN TRAN VU

The Tran Vu Temple (also known as Quan Thanh), the most important Taoist temple in Hanoi, was built in 1010 outside the city gates and is dedicated to demonic sorcerer god Huyen Thien Tran Vu. The bronze version of Tran Vu, almost two metres in height and weighing nearly four tons, dates from 1677. However, since its most recent restoration, the "Dark Warrior" appears more pop-arty than terrifying. *Daily 8am–6pm | admission approx. £0.40 | Quan Thanh, on the southeastern shore of the West Lake | ⊙ 30 mins | ▥ h1*

EATING & DRINKING

There are a number of good food stalls on the western edge of the *Old Quarter* in *Tong Duy Tan* and *Cam Chi*, about 500m northeast of the train station. Outside the Old Quarter, there are food and *pho* soup stalls, in *Le Van Huu (▥ k–l5)*, for example. Many restaurants in Hanoi are closed between 2pm and 6pm.

BUN CHA DAC KIM

One of Hanoi's top food stands – try the *bun cha* (pork meatballs with rice noodles) and the delicious *nem* (spring rolls). *1 Hang Manh | £ | ▥ j3*

CAFÉ BAR NOLA

This three-floor artsy café with a rooftop terrace is hidden away in a courtyard. Sit back and relax with a good cup of coffee, wine or cocktails. A few snacks and some simple dishes, plus WiFi, are also available. *89 Ma May | tel. 024 39 26 46 69, mobile 093 4 68 84 11 | £ | ▥ k3*

CONG CAPHE

The trendy café with vintage design impresses with its communist chic – with "bullet holes", black-and-white photos and colourful propaganda posters. The waiting staff wear camouflage. You wouldn't be surprised if a camera crew suddenly appeared to film a Viet Cong film. Of course, they serve stimulants: you should definitely try the coconut iced coffee! *101 Hoang Cau and 8 Thai Ha | tel. 024 37 33 99 66 | congcaphe.com | £ | ▥ 0*

INSIDER TIP
Coconut coffee treat

FOODSHOP 45

Well away from all the traffic, the idyllic Lake Truc Bach is the perfect place to take a quiet stroll – you can even hear the birds singing... and then sample the best Indian food in north Vietnam courtesy of the two brothers, Cuong and Hue. Relaxed atmosphere with sunset views. The veranda on the second floor is beautiful: you reach it from the circular staircase behind the curtain; it's only accessible in the evenings. *59 Truc Bach, near West Lake | tel. 024 37 16 29 59 | foodshop45. com | £ | ▥ h1*

INSIDER TIP
Romantic dining spot

HANOI SOCIAL CLUB

The social club near Hoan Kiem Lake is a trendy oasis across three whole floors, plus a jungle-like roof terrace. Even

INSIDER TIP
Cuban-style setting

inside, you could imagine you were in Cuba if it weren't for the throng of mopeds outside the door and Vietnamese musicians playing improvised music – it's nothing like salsa music! They serve good cocktails as well as muesli, pasta and snacks for those who are hungry. The atmosphere is somewhere between cool and cosy. *6 Ngo Hoi Vu | tel. 024 39 38 21 17 | FB: TheHanoiSocialClub | £ | ▢ j4*

HIGHWAY 4

Café bar with the best self-distilled brandies in the whole of Vietnam. Marvellous north Vietnamese cuisine, including specialities from the hill tribes. Cookery courses. Several branches. *5 Hang Tre | tel. 024 39 26 42 00 | FB: Highway4HangTre | ££ | ▢ k3*

LE BON STEAK HOUSE

This pleasant garden restaurant with a spacious interior offers international dishes, juicy steaks, salads and a breakfast buffet. Unfortunately, wine can only be ordered by the bottle. Live music from 9pm. *1 Pham Ngu Lao | tel. 024 39 33 88 66 | lebonsteak.com. vn | ££ | ▢ l4*

SHOPPING

Hang Gai, Hang Bong and Hang Trong are streets in the *Old Quarter* with many tailors and shops selling silk products. Hang Gai and Hang Bom, near St Joseph's Cathedral, also specialise in galleries and crafts. In Na Tho and Hang Trong, you'll find some rather expensive boutiques, while Luong Van Can is the place for bespoke *ao dais*, the traditional dress of

Economic boom meets traditional living in Old Hanoi

Vietnamese women. Hang Bac is known for silverware, jewellery, propaganda posters and crafts from the hill tribes, Lan Ong specialises in herbal remedies, and you'll find sweets in Hang Buom.

CRAFT LINK & HOA SEN GALLERY

Here you can buy crafts (especially woven fabrics from the hill tribes) and

Other vendors of these trendy souvenirs can be found at Hang Bac and Hang Be. *62 Hang Buom | ⫘ k3*

MEKONG QUILTS

Wonderful wall and bed covers; pillows, hammocks and baskets made from water hyacinth; plus bamboo bike frames. Everything here is handmade by under-privileged women.

Red is the colour of luck: bright souvenirs in Hanoi's Old Quarter

beautiful souvenirs. The proceeds go to projects supporting minorities and Hanoi street children. *43–51 Van Mieu, near Van Mieu Temple | craftlink.com.vn | ⫘ h4*

DONG XUAN MARKET 👣

The huge indoor market sells hats, shirts, fruit, vegetables, karaoke systems and much more – until midnight. *⫘ j2*

HANOI GALLERY

Colourful galleries lie around every corner in the old part of town. This one specialises in propaganda posters.

13 Hang Bac, Old Town | mekongquilts. com | ⫘ k3

SPORT & ACTIVITIES

Book organised excursions and tours to Hanoi's surroundings with *Ocean Tours (⫘ j1) (44 Nguyen Truong To | Bezirk Ba Dinh | tel. 024 39 26 04 63 | FB: oceantoursofficial)*. It's a reliable tour operator, especially for young people, with parties, campfires and kayaking adventures. *Todeco (⫘ j2–3) (91a/5 Ly Nam De | tel. 024 62 68 01 95 | mobile 090 3 22 70 82 | todeco-vn.com)* offers customised tours with English-speaking tour guides. The volunteers' association ★ Hanoi e.Buddies (hanoiebuddies. vn) offers free tours in Hanoi. The students show sides of the city seldom seen by tourists and get to practise their (good) English at the same time.

NIGHTLIFE

It's all the rage to mix with the locals in the bia hoi bars – Vietnamese beer costs less than 50p here, so sit in the plastic chairs and take in the busy atmosphere of the Old Quarter.

BAR & JAZZ CLUB MINH'S
Bar owner Minh teaches saxophone at the Hanoi Conservatory, so you can expect some high-class live jazz here (daily from 9pm). 1 Trang Tien | minhjazzvietnam.com | ⫟ I4

HANOI ROCK CITY
This place is a concert venue, bar and beer garden. Western bands play their music here, too, with jazz every Tuesday and everything from punk to hip hop at the weekend. Things get going at around 10pm (free entry until then). 27/52 To Ngoc Van | Tay Ho district | FB: hanoirockcity. welive | ⫟ 0

IBIERO CRAFT BEER STATION
The Vietnamese are famous for their breweries. Local light craft beers are increasingly being served in more trendy bars. They contain plenty of unusual botanicals, such as lemongrass, strawberries or mulberries, and can be chocolate brown or chilli hot,

sour or smoky. 99 Le Duan | opposite main train station | ibiero.com | ⫟ h4

OPERA HOUSE
The programme includes classical concerts, theatre performances (often in Vietnamese) and dance. For up-to-date listings, see, for example, Vietnam News. Tickets from approx. £7 | 1 Trang Tien | tel. 024 39 33 01 13 | hanoioperahouse.org.vn | ⫟ I4

THE SUMMIT LOUNGE
This open-air bar on the 20th floor of the Pan Pacific Hanoi is truly excellent and has the best view of the West Lake. Is it even necessary to point out that the prices reach lofty heights here too? 1 Thanh Nien | panpacific.com | ⫟ 0

TOP OF HANOI
Come here for sunset or to get away from the thick air. As you take your seat on the 65th floor of the Lotte Hotel, you'll be thinking, "This is the life." The later at night you go, the more the 360-degree panorama lights up. Sometimes DJ Xuxi plays a set (from 8.30 pm) and sometimes there are soul or rock acts. Tapas, pizza and burgers are served. 54 Lieu Giai, Ba Dinh district | lottehotel.com | ⫟ 0

WATER PUPPET THEATRE 🎭
Eleven actors operate the puppets to music from wooden flutes, gongs, drums and the dan bau, the single-string box zither. You can see a fisherman struggling with his catch, you hear the rice growing, watch a jaguar hunt ducks and encounter fire-breathing dragons. Performances

usually last for over an hour. Buy your tickets well in advance. Venues include *Thang Long Water Puppet Theatre* (*k3*) *(five shows daily 3–8pm | admission approx. £3.50–£7 | 57b Dinh Tien Doang | tel. 024 38 24 94 94 | thanglongwaterpuppet. org)* and the smaller *Lotus Water Puppet Theatre* (*I4*) *(admission approx. £3.50 | 16 Le Thai To | tel. 097 2 03 04 20)*

AROUND HANOI

1 HA LONG BAY ON LAND ★
90km south of Hanoi / 2hrs by car

Perfect fairy-tale scenery: wooded cone-shaped hills, rocky tips and mountain ridges rise abruptly from a sea of dark green. It's no surprise that the karst landscape here has become a top tourist attraction. The limestone formations, which have emerged over millennia, are comparable in beauty with Ha Long Bay — the difference being that there's no sea here.

In the heart of this spectacular landscape lies the provincial capital of *Ninh Binh (pop. 60,000)*. The town was formerly not much more than a pretty village, but that changed when independent travellers discovered the region. Today, the most popular spot is the town of *Tam Coc (admission approx. £4.20 | 10km west of Ninh Binh)*, where boats for tours along the river *(approx. £3.40/pers for a group of 4)* are moored.

The *Chua Bai Dinh Temple (daily 8am–5pm | 20km northwest of Ninh Binh | free admission, tower approx. £1.50, funicular approx. £1)* was built in 2003 and can be recognised from afar with its 11-storey tower. Lots of impressive buildings are found in this vast complex, the largest temple grounds in Vietnam (and it's not even finished yet), as well as thousands upon thousands of religious figures and Buddhas, 300 steps and a 360-degree panorama. Don't forget the 16m-high Sakyamuni Buddha – one of the largest in the country. *E4*

2 CUC PHUONG NATIONAL PARK
120km southwest of Hanoi / 2–2½ hrs by car

Vietnam's largest jungle national park. Here you can find some giant 1,000-year-old trees, squirrels, countless butterflies and hundreds of different bird species. The rocky outcrops rise to a height of 600m. No fewer than ten trekking trails crisscross this unique primeval forest. The Delacour's langur, originally thought to be extinct, was rediscovered here and is now bred in a small *monkey sanctuary (Endangered Primate Rescue Center, EPRC | daily 9–11am and 1.30–4pm | eprc.asia)*. Volunteers are welcome here to help secure the future of the primates. Facilities, including hotels, villas, a camp-site and restaurants (usually full at the weekend), are located in the park. October to December and March/April are the best months to visit. *Admission (with*

INSIDER TIP
Help the monkeys

guide for the EPRC) approx. £3 | tel.
024 22 43 16 42 | cucphuongnational
park.com | 𝄴 E3

🖪 HUONG TICH SON ★
*60km southwest of Hanoi / 2 hrs
by car*

It's about to get mystical: hidden away in *Huong Tich Son* (Mountain of Fragrant Vestiges) is the Huong Tich Cave with the *Perfume Pagoda (Chua Huong)*, which was built in honour of the goddess of mercy, Quan Am. You have to experience Vietnam's number one place of pilgrimage – but if possible, don't go for the New Year festival! Then, up to 60,000 visitors daily are rowed in 5,000 boats to the magnificent limestone site. These numbers put a distinct damper on the romantic atmosphere; or rather, romance gets lost amid a traffic jam on the river and the busyness of the festival. Any time of year, you have to take a boat to get to the pagoda. The best thing to do is to visit on a day trip from Hanoi *(from approx. £11)*. A cable car takes visitors up to the pagoda and grotto on the mountain. Alternatively, you can make the strenuous, two-hour climb (sturdy shoes essential). 𝄴 E3

🖪 CHUA TAY PHUONG & CHUA THAY
40km west of Hanoi / 1 hr by car

Situated in the heart of a fertile rice-growing area around 40km west of Hanoi, are these two magnificent pagodas, only a few kilometres apart from each other.

The *Chua Tay Phuong* near the village of Thach Xa stands on a hillock, but to reach it you will have to climb around 260 steps. The three ironwood buildings have elegant upward-sweeping eaves, beautifully adorned with all kinds of dragons and other mythical creatures – phoenix, *ky lan* (a unicorn-like beast) and turtles. Visitors also get to admire 62 precious statues, among them the 18 *la han* ("enlight-

Active and lively in Cuc Phuong National Park: a Delacour's langur

ened ones"), masterfully carved from the wood of the jackfruit tree.

Situated by Lake Long Tri near the village of Sai Son, at the foot of a limestone peak and surrounded by temples and pavilions, is *Chua Thay* or the "Master's Pagoda". It is dedicated to the miracle-worker and sorcerer, Tu Dao, who withdrew to the mountain in the 12th century to meditate and to disseminate the teachings of the Buddha. Tu Dao is also the patron saint of water puppeteers. *Admission approx. £0.85/pers | ⏱ approx. 30 mins each | 🕮 E3*

🔳 HOA BINH

75km southwest of Hanoi / 1½–2 hrs by car

Hoa Binh is a rather nondescript provincial capital, with hidden beauty in its surroundings. Most of the visitors are locals, who come to these parts to explore the Muong hill tribe's villages, such as *Ban Dam* and *Giang Mo*, and to admire the impressive, stilted longhouses. The *Mai Chau valley* is home to the Tai Don and Tai Dam peoples. It's best to visit their villages with a guide (up to approx. £8.50) *🕮 E3*.

🔳 BACH LONG GLASS BRIDGE (WHITE DRAGON) ★ 👥

Moc Chau, 200km west of Hanoi / 4½ hrs by car

The "White Dragon" is not only appealing to those who love architecture. If you're not afraid of heights, you can stroll along the delicate glass suspension bridge over the rugged mountain valley in the Son La province near Moc Chau, with a maximum of 449 other people. You will enjoy a truly spectacular panoramic view, accompanied by an adrenaline rush from the dizzying height. According to the *Guinness Book of World Records*, it is currently the longest glass bridge in the world at 632m. The bridge is an architectural masterpiece made of specially hardened glass and steel. Those wearing high heels will be passed slippers, which are also really practical for walking on the smooth glass when it's raining. *Daily 7am–10pm | admission approx. £24 | FB: caukinhbachlong mocchauisland | ⏱ 2–4 hrs | 🕮 D3*

🔳 DUONG LAM

50km northwest of Hanoi / 1 hr by car

For over 1,200 years, the Red River Delta has been home to a unique cultural landscape. The heritage-protected village of Duong Lam (near Son Tay) lies amid rice fields, embankments and dams: a collection of 140 traditional houses dating from the early 16th century. Some families are said to have been here for 400 years, including Chin Giap's family, now in its 12th generation. You can stop by for lunch with some of the residents or sleep in a homestay. Wander through the ivy-clad alleyways – some of which are surrounded by metre-high, weathered ruins – from the

> **INSIDER TIP**
> **Genealogy and lunch**

temple to the meeting hall, through archways with brick roofs and inner courtyards. The renovated *Dinh Mong Phu* (a community house from 1533, expanded in 1859) has a beautifully decorated roof and historic woodcuts. You can visit two magnificent tombs of kings who came from the village: Phung Hung (761–802) and Ngo Quyen (897–944). *Admission to the village approx. £1 | ⏱ 3 hrs | ▥ E3*

HA LONG BAY

(▥ F3) **A night by the legendary** ★ **Ha Long Bay: on the horizon, a caravan of hunchbacked elephants appears to move past the anchored junks and tourist boats; move slightly closer, and silent sentinels seem to stand guard in the pale moonlight.**

The swirling mists in the winter months can certainly fire the imagination! Around 2,000 islands emerge in all forms and sizes from the waters of the Gulf of Tonkin. There are two possible explanations for their creation. Firstly, a scientific one, which suggests that the rocks were part of the southwestern Chinese limestone plateau, which was flooded by the sea after the last Ice Age. And then a legend – one of many: to fend off Mongol cavalry, a dragon flew down from the sky and destroyed the landscape with its flailing tail. The dragon then dived into the sea, so the water would flood the valley.

What used to be two idyllic fishing ports, *Hon Gai* and *Bai Chay*, are now together called *Ha Long City* and are connected by a bridge. They have merged to become one large and lively resort, with an ever-expanding skyline of hotels, a night market, a casino, an over-priced water puppet theatre, a giant circus arena and *Paradise Marina*, 5km away on the *Tuan Chau Peninsula*. And, of course, you can take a funicular over the bay to the Ba Deo mountain and the *Sun*

Ha Long Bay makes the perfect setting for exciting legends

World Theme Park (approx. £12 | from Hon Gai | halong.sunworld.vn), with a big wheel and waxwork museum.

SIGHTSEEING

CAVES

The attraction of Ha Long Bay lies primarily in the countless dripstone caves that can be explored as part of a boat tour. The *Hang Dau Go* or "Cave of Wooden Stakes" is so named because during the 13th century it was used as a hiding place for a large collection of sharp wooden weapons, which the northern Vietnamese people used to put 500,000 Mongols under Kublai Khan to flight. The cave is reached via 90 steps. Do also try to visit *Hang Trong*, the "Drum Cave". Wind and weather cause the dripstones to emit unique noises. The finest cave of all is the strikingly illuminated *Hang Sung Sot*. The tour groups are dispersed around the three vast chambers; this way they can enjoy the circular tour with its almost mystical vistas in relative peace. Boat tours start in Bai Chay, Hon Gai, Tuan Chau or from Cat Ba Island. *Admission per cave approx. £0.85–£1.70*

FLOATING VILLAGES

What amazing waterborne activity! In huge Ha Long Bay, an area of 1,500 km², more than 1,600 people live on and earn their living from the water. There are only four settlements, including the largest floating villages in Asia, which are hidden between the distinctive limestone islands, such as *Cua Van* near Cat Ba. This is a spectacular place to live – apart from the expensive electricity for diesel generators and the storms during the typhoon season. When storms happen, the houseboats, pontoons and wooden living huts are tied together and taken to a bay offering more protection. The residents in Cua Van, Van Gia or Vong Vieng mainly earn their livelihood from breeding fish, which live directly beneath their houses. Others fish for squid at night, and pearl breeding also depends on floating pearl farms. The village shop is a wooden floating motorboat with a canopy, and even the doctor arrives in a rowing boat. The mayor's house and school are all floating. The villages are on the excursion schedules of some Ha Long tour operators, such as *Paradise Cruises (Thuan Chai | para disecruise.com)*.

EATING & DRINKING

HONG HANH

You should be happy if you get a table here – the locals know where to find a good and reasonably priced meal. Choose your own fish or lobster from the tanks with the waitress and know that your food is nothing but fresh. There are two branches. *442 Nguyen Van Cu | tel. 020 33 83 58 92; 50 Ha Long | tel. 020 33 81 23 45 | both: Bai Chay | ££*

SHOPPING

NIGHT MARKET IN BAI CHAY

Piled high on the tables between the promenade and beach are chopsticks, swimwear, shoes, toys and knick-knacks of all kinds. And there's a small  funfair for children. *Daily 6–11pm*

SPORT & ACTIVITIES

BOAT TRIPS

For trips out on to Ha Long Bay and to Cat Ba Island, go to the tourist pier in *Bai Chay* (near the Thang Long Hotel) for tickets and boats *(from approx. £43 per boat per day, additional price approx. £5, plus accommodation fee of approx. £7–£13 for 1–3 nights).* Waiting for passengers to arrive are some 400 or so boats, junks and paddle steamers from all price ranges. Starting in Hanoi, there are three-day trips with accommodation from £50 (from about 12 people, often also including a party …). Ha Long tours also leave from Cat Ba. Because all boats can now anchor in one bay, you

have to be prepared for plenty of die-sel fumes and karaoke-style speaker systems.

KAYAKING TOURS

If you want to do more than just swim around the bay, you can explore some of the caves by taking a kayak through a narrow opening and then paddling into the emerald green lagoon, for example in *Hang Luon Cave*. Or you can make a detour to the "floating" fishing villages, such as *Van Gia*.

NIGHTLIFE

TRUNG NGUYEN 2

It's impossible to overlook or ignore this bar above the main road. A popu-lar place to chat over fruit juices, beer, whisky, ice cream and snacks. *Ha Long Road (promenade) | Bai Chay | £*

A wonderful world made of rock: a light show in the Hang Sung Sot cave

AROUND HA LONG BAY

⑧ CAT BA

20km southwest of Ha Long City / 1 hr by boat

Ready for an island? Cat Ba is the largest island in Ha Long Bay and is just a (cat) leap from Ha Long City. Especially in the main town, *Cat Ba*, small hotels abound, as at weekends it is the preferred destination for countless trippers, seeking the pleasures of the karaoke bars. However, a large part of the island has been designated as a conservation area, so there are limits on how far the tourist developments can go. Wooded slopes extending to a height of 300m, deep gorges, caves and grottos, as well as beaches enclosed by rocks, form a small, South Pacific-style area, a perfect habitat for monkeys and bird species. The best time of year for swimming in the sea is from June to October; at other times it is often cool and misty. If you join a tour of the national park, you can visit caves where stone implements and human bones thought to be up to 7,000 years old were *found (admission approx. £1.30)*.

The *Sky Bar* in the *Sea Pearl Hotel (219, 1/4 Road | waterside promenade | FB: seapearlhotelcatba | ££)* boasts a cool rooftop pool and a panoramic view from the 11th floor, as well as ice-cold drinks. Or perhaps you want to sing: in the chic venue *Marigold (173–174, 1/4 Road, waterside promenade | tel. 090 4 35 55 86 | marigoldcatba.com | ££),* you can oil your vocal cords on the roof terrace with seafood by the kilogramme – and then head for the venue's karaoke bar. Definitely a must for an authentic Vietnam experience! *(⊞ F3)*

INSIDER TIP
A star is born

⑨ HAI PHONG

45km southwest of Ha Long City / 1 hr by car

Vietnam's third largest city (pop. 900,000) has kept its colonial charm in some of its districts: this is down to the French, who promoted the port's reconstruction here, about 100km southeast of Hanoi, from 1876. Today, in the *Quartier Français* you can see delightful architectural gems from the period around 1900, such as the theatre, observatory, city museum, station and post office. Around Dien Bien Phu you will find villas, hotels and colonnades adjoining the Old Town. In the pretty, 18th-century *Den Nghe Temple (corner of Le Chan/Me Linh),* you can see a richly ornamented stone altar; the gilded palanquins date from the 19th century, as do the gold furnishings. In the evenings you can go to the *Gentleman Lounge (64 Dien Bien Phu | FB: gentlemanlounge)* at the Manoir Des Arts hotel to enjoy a glass of wine with classical music or jazz, and a mixed-demographic audience. Ferries leave from *Ben Binh Terminal* several times a day to go to *Cat Ba Island (slow boat 2 hrs, hydrofoil approx. 30 mins).* ⊞ F3

Shops on the water: selling groceries in Ha Long Bay

🔟 BAI TU LONG BAY

*20km north of Ha Long City /
3 hrs by boat*

Apart from the endless trail of boats, this northern bay is much quieter than Ha Long Bay. There are not so many spectacular caves, but instead you will find several largeish beaches, such as on the islands of *Quan Lan* and *Van Don*. King prawns and fish are farmed on Quan Lan and you can still witness some of the surviving traditions, such as the boat races that form part of the village festival in the summer. But as you walk the streets and explore the main village, you will see men at work sawing and hammering. Once the first bungalows are finished, there are bound to be more – on both islands' beaches. Several ferries per day run from Cam Pha/Cai Rong on the mainland to Quan Lan; they also leave from Hon Gai (Ha Long City).

The island of Van Don further north is connected to the mainland by a bridge. There are two ferries a day from Quan Lan, or you can catch the hydrofoil from Ha Long City. At *Bai Dai Beach* at the eastern end of Van Don, it's still quite rural, but here too you can't miss all the new building work taking place along this part of the coast. An endless stream of freighters, boats and ferries make their way across the bay against the magnificent backdrop of rocky islets. In fact, Van Don was a fishing port as many as 1,000 years ago.

Taking the lead from young Vietnamese people and honeymoon-ers, globetrotters are now going off the beaten track away from Van Do to the main island of *Co To (50km from Ha Long City | 25 km / 1 ½ hrs by speedboat from Van Don island)*, with its excellent beaches and photo-worthy steep rocks. It's just the right place for anyone wanting to experience an authentic part of Vietnam and wanting to have fun in the sun too, with fresh seafood barbecued right on the beach. The island can look different according to the time of year: during the Vietnamese holiday season and on national holidays (especially April–July and December), it is bustling with karaoke singers. At other times, you can enjoy a quieter time with empty beaches. *F–G3*

INSIDER TIP
BBQ on the beach

SA PA

(□ C2) **Follow hair-raising bends and endless zigzags through the majestic mountain landscape surrounding ★ ▐ Sa Pa. Here, the colourful world of the hill tribes awaits you.**

Sa Pa (pop. 40,000) was developed by the French about 100 years ago as a spa and military sanatorium. Pretty villas, fortress-like country houses and a church recall the colonial era. Although the town is a remote spot and the coldest and mistiest place in Vietnam (best time to visit is September–November), it has become a bustling tourist destination.

The little town is spread across hilly terrain at a height of 1,560m, at the foot of the Fan Si Pan (Phan Si Pang), a mountain often shrouded in low cloud. The Hoang Lien Son range forms a backdrop. Among the long-standing traditions of the hill tribes are the construction of stilt houses, a belief in natural spirits, betel nut chewing, tooth blackening and eyebrow shaving. Many of the people here no longer wear the colourfully embroidered traditional dress with heavy silver jewellery – it is mostly only women who still wear this clothing, and often only on market days or holidays.

The usual way to reach the town is by tourist or public bus from Hanoi (journey time 5–6 hours) or via Lao Cai (37km northeast of Sa Pa), reachable on the railway line built in 1922.

SIGHTSEEING

MARKETS

The *Sa Pa market (daily 7am–6pm | Dien Bien Phu | above Lake Sa Pa)* has moved into a two-storey hall. On the first floor, you will find lots of textiles and silver jewellery. There are other lively markets in the vicinity too, where people of the hill tribes meet each other (and don't just pose for photos for money like they do in Sa Pa).

Tribal women, most from the Black Hmong people, wander the streets and alleys of Sa Pa to sell their hand-embroidered goods and – quite often – photos with their children, to tourists. They have a good command of French and English, and deploy some sophisticated sales techniques.

EATING & DRINKING

SAPA SKY VIEW

It's best to come here before the trekking tours arrive, so you can allow your eyes to wander in peace around the greenest panoramic view of the hills and valleys – whether from the veranda or inside in this bar in the Chai Long Sapa hotel. By the way, it's also popular with wedding companies, so you may have to be prepared to enjoy some romantic music. *24 Dong Loi | tel. 091 4 60 25 29 | FB: skyview restaurantsapa | ££*

ACTIVITIES

FUNICULAR TO FAN SI PAN

The *Fan Si Pan (Phan Si Pang)*, at 3,143m Vietnam's highest mountain, is located in the north of *Hoang Lien Son Nature Reserve*, known mainly for its diverse bird species. Reaching it is now far less gruelling. Sa Pa has changed rapidly – it has embraced luxury! There are now rooftop pools. Instead of hole-in-the-ground pit toilets, there are now toilets with warmed seats. Instead of tea, Nescafé is served at homestays, and instead of exhausting treks lasting two to three days to Fan Si Pan, a cable car takes you there non-stop *(daily 8am–5.30pm, approx.*

You can walk to the foaming Cat Cat waterfall from Sa Pa

Green, blue, red, violet: traditional clothes at the Bac Ha market

£27/pers | *fansipanlegend.sunworld. vn).* It takes 20 minutes to reach the mountain station; from here, it's a 600-step climb to the summit.

WALKS TO HILL VILLAGES & WATERFALLS
Easy walks via suspension bridges and through terraced paddy fields lead into the surrounding countryside, including to the *Cat Cat waterfall (admission approx. £2.50 | 3km west of Sa Pa)* in a bamboo forest and the *Thac Bac* or "Silver" waterfall *(10km west of Sa Pa)*, which drops about 100m in three stages. The walks pass through hill tribe villages, where accommodation is available – for example, in *Ta Phin* (Village of the Red Dao) – or else you can take a stroll through the delightful Ta Van valley to the village of *Ta Van*. In the popular village of *Cat Cat* near Sa Pa (on the walk through the village you encounter the waterfall mentioned above), you can watch the Hmong women at work on their weaving and embroidery. Blue dresses and turban-style headwear are the characteristic features of Hmong clothing, which they still make themselves and dye with indigo.

THE HMONG SISTERS
Everyone comes together here at the end of the day: it's the only real bar in Sa Pa. Have fun by the fire with a mulled wine and water pipes, live bands and pool. *31 Muong Hoa | FB: Thehmongsisterssapa*

AROUND SA PA

🔟 MU CANG CHAI

160km southeast of Sa Pa / 3–3½ hrs by car

Away from the bustle of Sa Pa or Bac Ha, Yen Bai province along Road 32 has really spectacular views to offer: the green shimmering paddy terraces in Mu Cang Chai reach record heights. The Hmong farmers work on the narrow terraces at a dizzying height to plant the rice – remember to keep your balance! The best time to take photographs here is during the harvest, from September to the beginning of November, when the hill terraces and valley scenery light up in gold in the sun. An interesting detail: the rice has been watered for a long time using a famous invention made of halved bamboo stalks. 🎋 *D2*

> **INSIDER TIP**
> **Bathed in golden light**

🔢 BAC HA

100km north-east / 2½ hrs from Sa Pa by car

This small town (pop. 3,000) lies at an altitude of 900m. It's famed for its lively *market* – a sea of green, blue, red and violet – which draws tourists to the town on Sunday. Everyone wants to see and photograph the "Flower Hmong" *(Hmong Hoa)*, so called because of their multicoloured clothing adorned with floral motifs. 🎋 *D2*

CAO BANG

(🎋 E1) **Nestling between two rivers and high, craggy mountains, the capital of one of the most forested Vietnam provinces welcomes its visitors.**

🚩 Cao Bang (pop. 50,000) is a typical arid border town (it's close to China), but its surroundings are very green. The region is renowned for its rugged and wildly overgrown karst hills, free-flowing rivers and thick rainforests. A whole day is needed to cover the more than 270km north from Hanoi, and Cao Bang makes a good starting point for excursions to the impressive *Ban Doc waterfall* and the *Ba Be National Park*, the picturesque *Thang Hen lakes* (four-wheel drive required), the beautiful *Pac Bo cave* and the markets of the hill tribes.

The town and province is populated mainly by the Tay (Tho), but also by many Nung and some Hmong, who offer homestays.

EATING & DRINKING

There are a number of good, inexpensive food stalls in the market in *Hoang Nhu* for a quick meal.

PIZZA CHI

Who would have thought that sumptuous yet crispy wood-fired pizza is served up in the mountains of north Vietnam? Don't be deterred by the simple, tube-shaped look of the place! *81 Vuon Cam | tel. 0169 3 80 41 06 | £*

Tay women carry heavy loads on sticks across their shoulders

SHOPPING

With a little luck, you can buy finely woven, brightly coloured carpets made by the Tay and Muong ethnic groups in the markets. The carvings here are also of a very high quality. Markets are colourful, with very friendly traders and live stock markets including water buffalos. The large hill tribe market in *Tra Linh* on the N 3, held on the 4th, 9th, 14th, 19th, 24th and 29th day of the lunar month, is impressive.

AROUND CAO BANG

🔟 BA BE NATIONAL PARK
125km southwest of Cao Bang / 3½ hrs by car

Now for the enchanted fairy tale – and above all tranquillity and solitude: the gigantic limestone mountains on the country's largest lake protrude almost vertically out of the water. It's not surprising that the area is also called the

"Ha Long Bay of the Mountains". The lake stretches for over 8km, and the mountains, over 1,500m high, and deep valleys make the scenery picture perfect. In the surrounding tropical rainforest around 300 animal species thrive, including threatened species like the leaf monkey – the diversity here is incredible. A memorable experience is a boat trip through the nearly 30m-high, 300m-long *Puong Cave*. It is home to countless bats, and the rocks and stalactites look eerie in torchlight. Three-day tours from Hanoi cost around £215 per person (for two people), for example from *Asiatica Travel (asiatica-travel.de)* or from the busy Mr Linh from *Ha Giang Trails (mobile 093 6 48 90 68, tel. in Hanoi 024 36 42 54 20 | hagiangtrails.com)*, which also offers a homestay in Coc Toc and treks through the jungle. You have to pay a fee of approx. £1.70 at the visitor centre at the park gate. *National Park Office tel. 020 93 89 41 26 | ⌖ E2*

INSIDER TIP
Jungle adventures

🖈 HANG PAC BO
50km northwest of Cao Bang / 1½ hrs by car

On the Ho Chi Minh trail: the "birthplace of the revolution" can be found at the dream-like *Hang Pac Bo* cave (also known as *Hang Coc Bo*) in Truong Ha village near the border with China. Ho Chi Minh (called Nguyen Ai Quoc at the time) crossed the border from China and lived and worked here in 1941, during the Second World War, when Vietnam was occupied by Japan. He finally declared Vietnam's independence from France in 1945.

Proof of his time here is provided by personal objects, such as a typewriter, pistol and case, a wooden bedframe and a boulder, on which the Vietnamese leader of the revolution is said to have translated the history of the Communist Party of the Soviet Union into Vietnamese and written poems. The government in exile also had its headquarters here during the First Indochina War against the French between 1946 and 1954. Cao Bang province was one of the first regions to be completely freed from French colonial rule. The 🐷 *memorial and museum (daily 7.30–11.30am, 1.30–4.30pm | free admission | ⏱ 1 hr)* is often visited by locals. ⌖ E1

🖈 BAN DOC WATERFALL
85km northeast of Cao Bang / 2½ hrs by car

A tumbling cascade: the *Ban Doc waterfall* (also known as the *Ban Gioc waterfall*) at Trung Khanh is one of the prettiest and largest in the country and its water rushes down into the rugged mountainous landscape over its 300m-wide rocky crest at three levels, when it's at its most stunning at the end of the rainy season, around September. A few kilometres before it, you can visit the 🐷 *Tiger Cave (Hang Nguom Ngao | daily 8am–5pm | free admission). Waterfall daily 8am–5pm | admission approx. £1.70 | ⏱ 30 mins | ⌖ F1*

HA GIANG

(□ D1) **In a rugged, remote landscape amid the furthest northern peaks of Vietnam, passes zig-zag around mountains: one turn round the steep rice terraces on the slopes is more beautiful than the next.**

The provincial capital Ha Giang (pop. approx. 40,000) on the banks of the Song Lo is considered by many travellers as a place to travel through, especially for (experienced!) motorcyclists on their way to the *Ha Giang Loop* near the border with China, a dream stretch with endless snaking roads, where the mountains stand like huge pointed caps. The passes here get called *quan ba*, "heaven's gates", because the areas around Ha Giang are home to some of the steepest and highest mountains in the country, such as the approximately 2,400m-high *Tay Con Linh* and *Kieu Lieu Ti*, which are sometimes covered with snow in the winter.

INSIDER TIP
Mountain rollercoaster

Members of the Tay, Dao and (White) Hmong, and ethnic splinter groups such as the San Diu, Lo Lo and Pu Peo, live in Ha Giang. They are all beginning to offer homestays more often (but be prepared that they tend to be of the sparser type).

The popular motorcycle routes in this challenging mountainous area take you, for example, to the (Sunday) markets where you'll see the hill peoples in their colourful traditional clothes.

The isolation, the bad road quality and the authorisation required to travel here kept this poor area away from the tourist trail and the changes that it brings. However, these times seem likely to be over soon as a big tourism offensive is being launched. Permits are still required for Quan Ba, Dong Van and Meo Vac. *Ha Giang Trails (hagiangtrails.com)* and hotels in Ha Giang can organise these for around £8.50.

EATING & DRINKING

GOLDEN BBQ

In this modern local, the meat is fried at the table, while you get hungrier and hungrier watching it. Try the delicious sushi while you wait. They also serve hot pots. *42A Nguyen Van Linh | tel. 094 3 91 29 92 | FB: Golden BBQ Ha Giang | £*

AROUND HA GIANG

🔟 DONG VAN

140km northeast of Ha Giang / 4–5 hrs by car

The route over the Quan Ba Pass, with a magnificent backdrop of mountains, takes you to Dong Van, the northernmost area of Vietnam. In the morning, the traditional 📢 loudspeaker system still rings out through the streets, something that has long been a thing of the past in many tourist areas of Vietnam. The 🐗 *Vuong Palace (daily*

8am–5pm | free admission | 15km southwest of Dong Van | ⏱ *1 hr)* in Sa Phin was once the residence of Vuong Chinh Duc, who became extremely rich from the opium trade. The estate, built in 1914, looks almost like a fortress in stone, clay and wood, with several levels of tiled roof, watch towers and three inner courtyards. In total, the palace has 64 rooms, which are adorned with excellent statues and wood cuttings. Today, the farmers here primarily grow rice and fruit (pears, peaches and apples). Ginseng, aniseed and cinnamon also grow in the gardens.

The simple local *Au Viet (in Dong Van, To 3, near the market | tel. 094 2 90 58 88)* serves a western breakfast (eggs, baguettes), hot pots, noodle soups, coffee and beer. 🗺 *E1*

🔢 MEO VAC

170km northeast of Ha Giang / 5–6 hrs by car

Dong Van leads southeast to Meo Vac along 25km of breathtakingly narrow hairpin bends through the karst landscape of the *Dong Van Plateau (dongvangeopark.com)*, a UNESCO Global Geopark. The journey takes you almost up into the clouds, through rugged limestone scenery, a deep ravine over the *Nho Que River* and through the spectacular *Ma Pi Leng Pass* at 1,500m – many think this is the most beautiful stretch in Vietnam! 🗺 *E1*

Dramatic scenery: the karst landscape on Dong Van plateau

HUE &
CENTRAL
VIETNAM

VIETNAM'S TREASURE CHEST

The central region of Vietnam around the resort of Da Nang is home to three important historical sites. In addition to the old imperial city of Hue, with its Citadel by the Song Huong – the "Perfume River" – there are impressive imperial tombs and the enchanting ruins of the Champa complex in My Son.

Don't forget to visit the largely Chinese market town of Hoi An, from the 17th century onwards an internationally important trading port on the South China Sea. And if the region around Hue should

Walk into the "Forbidden City": the Imperial Palace in Hue

live up to its reputation as the wettest in Vietnam when you visit, simply head further south to the sunny beaches of Da Nang, via the Bach Ma mountains. The port city is also famous for the Cham Museum, which sheds light on the ancient civilisation that once flourished here.

During the Vietnam War, the magnificent Marble Mountains above Da Nang became a hideout for Viet Cong guerrillas. Thanks to its location at an altitude of 1,500m, Da Lat is described as the "City of Eternal Spring" for its pleasant, cool temperatures.

3 Phong Nha-Ke Bang National Park

China Beach

7 Tra Que Vegetable Village

Cua Dai Beach

Hoi An ★ p. 83

Vĩnh An

An Hải

Quảng Ngãi

Long Thành

(1A)

Phù Mỹ

An Nhơn

Quy Nhơn

Sông Cầu

Lá Hai

Tuy Hòa

Hòa Vinh

M'Đrắk

Ninh Hòa

(1A)

Nha Trang

Cam Ranh

Tân Sơn

Lợi Hải

8 **Po Klong Garai Towers ★**

S o u t h

C h i n a   S e a

MARCO POLO HIGHLIGHTS

★ **HUE CITADEL**
The opulence and grandeur of Vietnam's former rulers ➤ p. 72

★ **CHAM MUSEUM**
Relics from an ancient and unique culture in Da Nang ➤ p. 80

★ **MY SON**
In the middle of the jungle: the ruins of a Cham temple complex ➤ p. 82

★ **MARBLE MOUNTAINS**
Mysterious caves and pagodas — plus a fantastic all-round view from Mount Thuy Son ➤ p. 82

★ **HOI AN**
Picturesque rows of streets in the Old Quarter, plus much Chinese- and Japanese-style charm ➤ p. 83

★ **DA LAT**
The lovers' city oozes colonial charm, while the surrounding area is a haven for adventure-sports enthusiasts ➤ p. 89

★ **PO KLONG GARAI TOWERS**
The Cham perfected the art of temple construction ➤ p. 90

50 km
31.06 mi

HUE

(🗺 G7) **In Hue, you can slip into an imperial robe – and you're ready to travel back in time!**

In the old imperial city, you can follow the trail of noble rulers in their palaces or see them enjoying a banquet at a royal dinner – but the beach is not far away.

Hue (pop. 400,000) was the capital of the last imperial dynasty, the Nguyen, from 1802 to 1945. As the city lies about halfway between Hanoi and Ho Chi Minh City, it has developed into an important hub for central Vietnam. Another factor that has contributed to the city's appeal is its idyllic location straddling the Song Huong (Perfume River), which flows at a sluggish pace flanked by gentle hills. One theory about the origin of its evocative name refers to the sweet-smelling hardwood logs that were once transported on the river. Another theory is

that in spring, blossom lands on the river. Modern Hue has retained its traditional importance as an administrative centre and seat of learning. And last, but not least, Hue's friendly, outward-looking residents play their part in creating a welcoming atmosphere in the city.

SIGHTSEEING

CITADEL ★

On the northern bank of the Song Huong stands the 17th-century Citadel: you're lucky if you catch the morning changing of the guard (9am) or one of the irregular (evening) shows at the Noontime Gate – with dancers, elephants and martial arts. This fires the imagination, and it's helpful because over the centuries, the battles and bombs, fire and typhoons have left comparatively little of the Citadel's original grandeur intact. To be honest, Hue's Citadel is no Vietnamese Versailles, but UNESCO has nevertheless reconstructed the most important buildings one by one.

The Citadel is surrounded by a walled enclosure some 10km in length on ramparts 6m high. It was once a state within a city, with temples, official apartments, decorative gardens and broad, shaded boulevards. Everything was laid out strictly in accordance with the rules of feng shui. In fact, it's like a set of nested boxes – with the outer Citadel leading to the Imperial City. And within the Imperial City, at the Citadel's heart, is the old *Imperial Palace*, called the "Forbidden City", where the library, private

WHERE TO START?

When you arrive in Hue, take a stroll along the **Song Huong promenade**, past the park, the bridge, which is beautifully illuminated at night, and the Saigon Morin colonial-style hotel and cafés. Continue as far as the pier, where you'll find the dragon boats. From here, take a boat to the pagoda or cross to the other side of the river to the Imperial City by taxi or *cyclo*.

The changing of the guard brings an air of times gone by to Hue's Imperial City

reception rooms and temple halls are open to the public. Cross the *Phu Xuan Bridge* to reach the *Flag Tower* dating from 1809. Flying from it on public holidays is the yellow flag of the "Heavenly Dynasty". The sturdy *Ngo Mon Gate* (Noontime Gate) is the main way into the Imperial City. In the past only the emperor was allowed to use this entrance. On top of the gate is the *Ngu Phung*, the brick-tiled "Five Phoenix Belvedere". This was where the emperor appeared on important occasions. It was also where the last Nguyen emperor announced his abdication in 1945.

Cross a courtyard and the "Golden Water Bridge" *(Trung Dao)* to reach the *Dien Thai Hoa* throne palace, the "Palace of Supreme Harmony". Note

the dominant red and gold, the colours of the imperial family. The emperor would sit on a magnificently carved, gilded throne in the centre of the hall. With nine stelae dividing up the area, the "Ceremonial Court" was where the mandarins-in-waiting would stand according to their rank of civilian officials or top military brass. Pass through the "Golden Gateway" *(Dai Cung Mon)* into the "Palace of the Laws of Heaven", behind which stands the Imperial Palace proper. To the right and left of it, in the "Hall of Mandarins", officials prepared for an audience with the emperor. Today, visitors can dress up as officials *(approx. £1.30)*. Turn to the left and you will be standing in front of the emperor's private quarters. Eunuchs stood guard over the Imperial harem here. On the right, *performances of folk music (ca hue)* take place in the *Duyet Thi Duong Royal Theatre* in the morning and afternoon *(10am, 3pm | admission approx. £6.90).*

Leave the Imperial City via the East Gate *(Hien Nhan Mon)* and head towards the museum complex. The palace museum, the *Museum of Royal Antiquities (Tue–Sun 7am–5pm | admission included in Citadel ticket | 3 Le Truc)* was installed in the former *Long An Palace* not far from the southeastern corner of the wall. It houses furniture, clothing, porcelain and decorative objects from the palace. It is worth a visit if only to look at the well-proportioned wooden structure. Its frame is made from very hard iron-wood, while many carvings, including poems and lines of prose, adorn the beams and windows. *Citadel Summer daily 6.30am–5.30pm, otherwise 7am–5pm | admission approx. £6.90, combined ticket for all Hue sights, incl. the 3 most important emperors' graves approx. £20.50, valid for 2 days | hueworldheritage.org.vn | ⊙ approx. 2–4 hrs*

CUNG AN DINH

This modest palace is ideally suited to start the imperial tour, as even in those days there was a fusion of culinary customs, art and architecture – the entrance gate alone is a feast for the eyes in Far Eastern, Baroque gingerbread style! Behind it is a cultural mix of European and Vietnamese elements: Greek columns hold the balcony at the front, and a

The gates and temple halls of the Citadel of Hue are witness to past imperial power

precious French wall covering made of silk imitates paintings with floral motifs inside the building. The majestic An Dinh Residence (also known as Khai Tuong Lau, constructed 1916–18) has been restored by professionals from the German Conservation Restoration & Education Program (GCREP). It features fantastic stucco reliefs, ceiling paintings and frescoes, antique furniture and a garden. Emperor Khai Din used this palace outside the citadel as his private retreat, to smoke opium and drink cognac while playing cards. Later on, his son Bao Dai, the last Vietnamese emperor, lived here. *Daily 8am–5pm | admission approx. £1.60 | 150 Nguyen Hue and 179b Phan Dinh Pung | ⊙ 30 mins*

EATING & DRINKING

In Hue, there are *bun bo hue* eateries (for example, *11b Ly Thuong Kiet*) every few metres. You eat what arrives: a bowl of *bun bo hue,* beef and rice noodle soup in the Hue style (approx. £1). And what is *banh trang trung?* It's Vietnamese-style pizza: crispy, thin and made of rice dough. Another street-food trend is the crêpe-like 🍴 🚩 *banh ep* (with cucumbers, papaya and herbs), which is also popular with children. You can find this typical snack here for around £0.50, for example in the historic Phu Cat quarter: *20 and 44 Nguyen Du (a side street off Chi Lang Street)* and *14 Le Thanh Ton.*

ANCIENT HUE 🚩

Tourists eat like emperors here, in a classy imitation temple with a lush garden. You must try the nine-course *Royal Dinner. 4/4/8 Lane 35 | Pham Thi Lien | near Thien Mu Pagoda | 104/47 Kim Long | tel. 023 43 59 09 02 | ancienthue.com.vn | £££*

CAFE ON THU WHEELS

A meeting place for travellers. Offers a proper breakfast, good drinks and long opening times. They also organise motorcycle tours into the surrounding countryside. *3/34 Nguyen Tri Phuong | tel. 076 8 42 62 15 | FB: cafeonthu wheelshuevietnam | £*

TROPICAL GARDEN

Garden restaurant for tourists in the Hotel Quarter. Folkloric shows every day and popular classic Vietnamese dishes like *banh khoai* pancakes and various noodle dishes. *27 Chu Van An | tel. 023 43 84 71 43 | FB: @the tropicalgardenrestaurant | ££*

SHOPPING

At the weekend, *Vo Thi Sau* and *Chu Van An* transforms into a pedestrianised street with a night-time market, offering many eateries, bars, shops, music and street performances. On the right bank of the river, there are also a number of market stalls (vegetables, fruit, coffee) in *Phan Boi Chau,* in *Nguyen Con Tru (corner of Ba Trieu)* and in *Huong Vuong,* near the bus station. *Dong Ba market*, southeast of the Citadel on the left bank of the river, is the address if you fancy one of those typical Vietnamese rice straw hats.

Well-rounded: hats for farmers and tourists

TRUC CHI GARDEN

Absolutely delightful: *truc chi*, created by artist Phan Hai Bang with a combination of traditional paper production and printing techniques. The art lies in converting bamboo *(truc)* into ultra-thin paper *(chi)* and then giving it translucent stencil motifs using a water jet. This creates unique decorations, for example for umbrellas, murals, hats, kites, lanterns and fans. You can also

INSIDER TIP
Truc chi decorations

learn *truc chi* here. Have patience – kids are usually the real masters of this art! *4-hr courses, price depends on number of participants (approx. £30 with 8 participants) | 5 Thach Han | tel. 093 5 10 14 14 | FB: trucchigarden*

BEACHES

Thuan An beach is worth the 13km journey northeast beside a pretty lagoon (unfortunately it's often rather dirty). Those visiting the beach will find a few eateries, places to lie down and sunshades. The sand is like icing sugar and you can get cocktails on the beach. During the week, it's empty!

NIGHTLIFE

BROWN EYES BAR
A classic and still very popular club for people up to 25 years old. Western music and karaoke. *56 Chu Van An*

CAFÉ BAR MUC DONG
A small pavilion made of glass and bamboo on a pond with a beer garden. Classical concerts are held from 8pm – along with jazz and Latin music – and you can get snacks, ice cream and cocktails from the well-equipped bar. They also serve speciality coffees here, with roasts from all over the world. *41a Hung Vuong | cafe-muc-ong.business. site*

INSIDER TIP
Global coffee beans

DMZ BAR
Popular with backpackers and resident expats. *44 Le Loi | dmz.com.vn*

AROUND HUE

1 BACH MA NATIONAL PARK

40km southeast of Hue / 1 hr by car

Waterfalls, emerald-coloured natural pools and fantastic views (unless it's raining again). Either way, put on a waterproof rain jacket and get active with trekking, climbing, abseiling and other adventurous activities that children will also enjoy, such as the 🎯 *Five Lakes Trail* across two strenuous kilometres that also involves some climbing. Alternatively, you can take it at a more leisurely pace and hike through the national park to the impressive waterfalls, lakes and the 1,444m mountain peak. You should wear hiking boots and long socks for this hike – the rainforest leeches happily welcome every visitor. The park is usually full and noisy at weekends. Accommodation is available in six basic guesthouses *(£). National Park Office in Hue (tel. 05 43 89 73 60). March–Sept daily 7am–5pm, Oct–Feb 7.30am–4.30pm | admission approx. £1.70 (incl. hiking maps), guide approx. £17/day, driver/jeep on site approx. £25 | 5-hr tour from Hue from around £25 | bachmapark.com.vn |* 🗺 *G7*

2 CHUA THIEN MU

5km west of Hue / 20 mins by car or 45 mins by bicycle

A legend has grown up around the "Heavenly Lady Pagoda" west of the city on the northern bank of the Perfume River. It is said that in 1601 the figure of an elderly lady appeared on a hill before the founder of the Nguyen dynasty, Nguyen Hoang. She insisted that this place belonged to a deity and demanded that a pagoda be built here. Nguyen Hoang obeyed and the country and the Nguyen family prospered for hundreds of years. In 1844 Emperor Thieu Tri added the octagonal, 21m-high *Phuoc Duyen tower*, which has become a symbol for Hue. Buddha statues are distributed across seven levels. A monk named Thich Quang Duc, who practised in Thien Mu, caused a stir in 1963. He drove a light blue Austin car, now occupying a building to the rear of the pagoda, to Ho Chi Minh City and in protest at the cruelty of the South Vietnamese Diem regime set himself on fire before the world's press. 🕐 *30 mins | 🗺 G7*

3 PHONG NHA-KE BANG NATIONAL PARK

210 km northwest of Hue / 4–5 hrs by car/ or 1 hr by plane to Dong Hoi Airport

An enormous sensation awaits you near Dong Hoi in Ke Bang National Park: the largest cave system in the world. The walls of *Hang Son Doong* reach cathedral-like heights of around 200m. However, only very few experienced expedition tourists are admitted here every year (see Sport, p.32). Most visitors explore the main cave of *Phong Nha*, 1.5 km by foot or by boat on an underground river through 15 grottoes. The 🎯 *Hang Toi cave (Dark Cave)* is a buzzing playground of adventures for old and young at weekends, with banana boats, mud-slinging, water slides and zip lines. With a helmet and headtorch, you can discover *Thien Duong (Paradise Cave)*, which gets quieter and more challenging after the first kilometre. Tours in caves that are lesser known and have been recently opened are offered by *Phong Nha Farmstay* (see p. 32) in Cu Nam. *Jan, Sept caves may be closed. Otherwise daily approx. 7am–4pm | admission per cave from approx. £6 plus boat rides | all caves 45–65km northwest of Dong Hoi, near Son Trach | phong nhakebang.vn | ▢ E6*

IMPERIAL TOMBS
(LANG KHAI DINH)
7–14km south or southwest of Hue / 30–45 mins by boat/car, depending on site chosen

Don't expect the Taj Mahal! But you can definitely sense the pomp and flair of long forgotten times, a pinch of feng shui harmony and a feeling of slightly morbid romanticism at these tombs. All were built to a similar pattern. Most of them are enclosed by a wall and are surrounded by a courtyard where stone figures stand guard. A pavilion includes marble tablets engraved with the achievements of the deceased emperor. Near the pavilion is a temple for worshipping the imperial family and the mausoleum with the emperor's remains.

The Tomb of *Tu Duc* was built between 1864 and 1867. The complex, with a pond filled with water lilies and lotus plants, is located 7km from Hue. The emperor spent a lot of time here, devoting hours to poetry, chess and fishing. At the point where the two rivers, the Ta Trach and the Huu Trach, merge to form the Perfume River, some 12km from Hue, is the tomb of Emperor *Minh Mang* (1840–43). Work started on it after his death. Palace, pavilion and three gateways were built in a park around two lakes, evoking a sense of space and peace. Emperor *Khai Dinh's* tomb was built on Mount Chau between 1920 and 1931. Look carefully and you will see a fusion of Asian and European decorative features, testament to the emperor's interest in European culture; the multi-coloured ceramic mosaics add to the charm of the temple. The tombs of *Gia Long, Thieu Tri* and *Dong Khanh* are smaller and more modest.

There are organised tours that include the tombs in their itinerary, but if you want to avoid the crowds it is better to arrange your own tour in a hired boat along the Perfume River *(2 hrs, including the Thien Mu Pagoda (Chua Thien Mu) and Tomb of Minh Mang, approx. £8.50)*, possibly also including a taxi. Or, as the tombs are some distance apart, you can hire a private boat and put a bicycle on board. It only costs approx. £0.85 to hire a bike and you will find cycle hire outlets everywhere, but do check that the brakes are working properly! The immediate vicinity of the tombs can get very crowded, so try to make your visit early in the morning or early evening. *Summer daily 6.30am–5.30pm, otherwise 7am–5pm | admission to each tomb approx. £5 | ⏱ 30 mins–1 hr | ▢ G7*

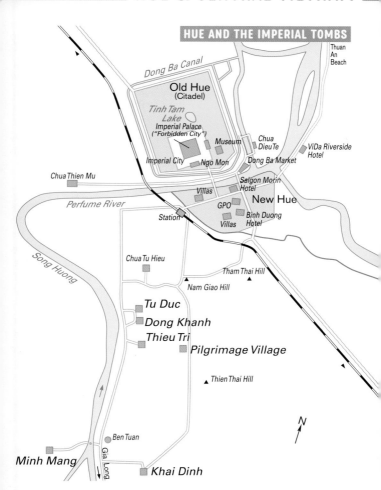

HUE AND THE IMPERIAL TOMBS

Thuan An Beach

Dong Ba Canal

Old Hue
(Citadel)

Tinh Tam Lake

Imperial Palace
(*"Forbidden City"*)

Museum

Chua DieuTe

ViDa Riverside Hotel

Imperial City

Ngo Mon

Dong Ba Market

Chua Thien Mu

Perfume River

Villas

Saigon Morin Hotel

New Hue

GPO

Station

Villas

Binh Duong Hotel

Song Huong

Chua Tu Hieu

Tham Thai Hill

Nam Giao Hill

Tu Duc

Dong Khanh

Thieu Tri

Pilgrimage Village

Thien Thai Hill

Ben Tuan

Gia Long

Minh Mang

Khai Dinh

N

DA NANG

(□□ G7) **Nobody passes through this hub quickly – Da Nang is the gateway to Hue, My Son and Hoi An. And the unique Cham Museum will even delight those who don't like museums!**

On the section of road from Hue you will notice a distinct change in the climate once you have negotiated *Cloud Pass (Deo Hai Van)*, which acts as a meteorological divide. You will soon reach Da Nang, the rapidly growing provincial capital of approx. 1.2 million inhabitants. Because of its location at the mouth of the River Han,

Da Nang has always been an important port. In 1965, the Americans occupied the town and set about developing what was to become one of their largest air bases in Southeast Asia. China Beach is renowned for its high waves – during the war American soldiers came here to surf when they had "rest and relaxation" time.

SIGHTSEEING

CHAM MUSEUM ★ 🛕
Prepare to experience a showcase of the gods, as three world religions meet in the Cham kingdom – Hinduism, Buddhism and Islam. But it's a peaceful place. Nevertheless, it's still an amazing puzzle: a god with an elephant head (Ganesha), female breasts as the "primeval mother" (Uroja), a phallus as god (Shiva). The religious art of the Cham created a mystical world, where Shiva dances, Vishnu meditates, lions and elephants unite to become remarkable mythical creatures, and the goddess of fertility looks on at all the chaos.

Founded in 1915 by the French, this small, but rather fine museum houses the world's best and largest collection of Cham artefacts, many of which are sandstone sculptures. No less than 800 years of civilisation are skilfully compressed into a tiny space. *Daily 7am–5pm | admission approx. £2 | near the Nu Vuong/Bach Dang junction | chammuseum.vn | ⏱ 2 hrs*

CAO DAI TEMPLE 🛕
Like the Holy See in Tay Ninh (see p. 109), the Cao Dai Temple here, the second-largest in the country, is an impressive sight. Access is strictly segregated by sex. Women enter the shrine on the left, men on the right. Priests are allowed to use the central entrance. Behind the altar the "divine eye" made from a huge glass ball watches the faithful at prayer. *Services daily 6am, noon, 6pm, midnight | admission free | near the station on Hai Phong | ⏱ 30 mins–1 hr*

EATING & DRINKING

BABYLON STEAKGARDEN 1 🍽
Not even fussy children will leave hungry here as the large menu includes both Vietnamese and western fare, such as pasta and fries. Speciality dishes include steaks and a barbecue with gigantic meat skewers cooked on the hot stone (for fewer fumes). *422 Vo Nguyen Giap | side of the beach near the Furama Resort | tel. 023 63 98 79 89 | FB: babylon steakgarden | ££*

TRUC LAM VIEN (GARDEN VIEW CAFÉ)

Bamboo garden retreat in imperial style with knotted trees, orchids and lanterns. They serve Vietnamese and Chinese specialities, noodle soups, hot pots, plus delicious seafood and western breakfasts with good coffee.

INSIDER TIP
Vietnamese buffet feast

At weekends in the evening, there is an almost endless buffet of Vietnamese delicacies to choose from – at a bargain price of under £7. *8–10 Tran Quy Cap | tel. 023 63 58 24 28 | truclamvien.com.vn | £–££*

BEACHES

China Beach, a popular spot with tourists, extends south from Mount Son Tra (Monkey Mountain) for about 30km. But take care as there are sometimes dangerous currents in these waters. The best time for swimming is from April to August.

The idyllic, but also treacherous, *Canh Duong Beach* near Lang Co, around 20km north of Da Nang, is about 8km in length. You can get to it by driving over the 496m-high *Hai Van Pass*. The "Ocean Cloud Pass", while often shrouded in cloud, may provide a dreamlike view of the peninsular, including the blue, shimmering lagoon.

The dance of the gods: sandstone carvings from the Cham Museum in Da Nang

NIGHTLIFE

SKY 21

See the moonlight and much more: enjoy cocktails here and listen to live music looking over rooftops and the sea. This is not the highest bar, but nor are the prices sky high here. If it rains, large umbrellas are opened; the pool beckons in sunny weather. Thursday from 5pm is *Ladies Night* with free drinks! Otherwise happy hour runs until 8pm. *Belle Maison Parosand Hotel, 216 Vo Nguyen Giap (beach promenade) | bellemaisonparosand. com/sky-21-bar*

AROUND DA NANG

4 MY SON ★

*70km southwest of Da Nang /
2–2½ hrs by car*

Just a heap of old ruins? Well, these ones are spectacular! Walk beneath the eyes of mythological creatures and gods through the sublime stillness of the temple ruins. From the fourth to the 13th century, My Son was the Champa people's religious and cultural centre. The founding of the shrine, dedicated to the god Shiva, is attributed to the Champa king Bhadravarman, whose power base was in present-day Tra Kieu, 20km to the east. In the seventh century, work started on replacing the sacred buildings, originally made of wood, with brick structures. No mortar or lime was used in their construction; remarkably, resin from the cau day tree held the walls together.

When the Viet Cong discovered the valley a thousand years later and considered it to be a safe hiding place, the US Army declared the region a "free fire zone". Only 20 of what was originally 70 sacred buildings survived the bombardment undamaged.

The temples, covered in moss and surrounded by dense jungle, and sitting beneath My Son mountain, are divided into four groups: Group A consists of the remnants of stone reliefs; Group B has a splendid gateway opening on to a shrine and a library adorned with frescoes of elephants.

The brick walls in the Group C buildings show predominantly Cham motifs like Shiva's lingam and the bull Nandi. Especially well preserved are the covered frescoes of Group D: an ensemble of six buildings and a stele courtyard with votive panels. Please note: countless landmines were laid around My Son and they are still live, so under no circumstances should you deviate from the marked trails! *Daily 6am–4.30pm | admission approx. £5 | ⏲ 2–4 hrs | 🗺 G7*

5 MARBLE MOUNTAINS ★

*8km southeast of Da Nang /
20 mins by car or moped*

Prepare to be enchanted: in the main cave of the Marble Mountains, you can experience the "illumination" of the Buddha – at noon, sunlight breaks through the holes in the cave roof and shines on the marble statue. The former hideaway of the Viet Cong is now lit with countless incense sticks. Here, Buddha, Quan Am and the rest watch over scores of (holiday) pilgrims from around the world. They climb up and down the steps; those who prefer not to walk can take the lift to the kingdom of the gods.

The cluster of five mountains near China Beach rise steeply from the plain. They are named after the five elements of Chinese philosophy: *thuy* (water), *tho* (earth), *kim* (metal), *moc* (wood) and *hoa* (fire). The most famous of the five is the "Water Mountain"; from the *Vong Giac Dai* viewpoint at the summit, there's a stunning panorama extending over the beach or, rather, the expanding skyline of hotel complexes, the sea and the other mountains. You can make a circular tour (torch and mosquito repellent spray essential) to explore the grottoes once used by the Cham and the impressive *Tam Tai Pagoda. Daily 8am–5pm | admission approx. £1.30,* ⛵ *free if you take the stairs | ⏱ 1–2 hours | 🗺 G7*

HOI AN

(🗺 G7) **The ultimate in kitsch. Some love the "romantic and picturesque" little town of** ⭐ **Hoi An, with its ancient Chinese charm of bygone days. Others can't get away soon enough from what they see as a hectic amusement park with an over-staged and pricey picture-book setting.**

As you stroll through alleys filled with lanterns, it's hard to imagine that some 300 years ago Hoi An (population 120,000), called Hai Pho (also Faifo) at the time, was one of the most important ports in Southeast Asia. It was established by the Cham and then extended by the Nguyen rulers. There are hardly any general stores left; outsiders have moved in and transformed the town into a collection of souvenir shops, restaurants and small hotels. Fortunately, Hoi An has retained its reputation as Vietnam's "tailor town", and you can get measured up for a shirt or blouse or silk suit or dress.

SIGHTSEEING

OLD QUARTER

The Old Quarter of Hoi An covers the area between the Bach Dang

This figure guards the Huyen Khong grotto with a stern expression

promenade and Phan Chu Trinh – if you take a stroll around the town, you will be inspired by the number of historic trading houses, assembly halls and pagodas – more than 800 buildings are historically important. The houses belonging to the Chinese community are particularly exotic. The Heavenly Empress Thien Hau, who watches over the fortunes of seafarers, is worshipped in the Phu Kien Pagoda in the Fujian Chinese assembly hall. Also of interest are the ornate carvings in the house of the Chaozhou Chinese.

An admission ticket is required if you wish to explore the Old Quarter, even if you just want to wander around in the evening without visiting the sites; a collective ticket is valid for five entries to the 23 historical sites and museums, but it is only valid for one day (approx. £5). They are available from one of several sales points in the Old Quarter, including opposite the Fujian Chinese assembly hall *(47 Tran Phu)*. Please refrain from smoking or wearing miniskirts, shorts, and tank tops in the pagodas and temples.

By day, Hoi An is certainly a town that draws you in. But on the 14th day of each month in the lunar calendar, it hosts a festival of lights: *Hoi An by Night*, when the narrow alleyways in the Old Quarter are illuminated by fairy lights, candles and lanterns. The townsfolk spend the evening in the old houses, listening to folk music, readings and sharing local delicacies.

INSIDER TIP
Hoi An by Night

JAPANESE BRIDGE

In Hoi An, the Chinese and the Japanese communities each had their own quarters, with the boundary line between the two zones an 18m-long covered Japanese bridge. Work on the first bridge (subsequently destroyed several times) started in 1593 in the Chinese Year of the Monkey, as is indicated by the two monkeys on the Japanese side of the bridge. Two years later, the wooden structure with a roof of green and yellow tiles was finished in the Year of the Dog. Note the two stone dogs on the Chinese side. ⊙ *10 mins*

TRADING HOUSES

Most of the commercial properties in the town date from the early 19th century. Today, they are still used for ancestor worship, business and family life. Probably the finest is *Quan Thang House (77 Tran Phu)*, with its striking green tile roof. *Phung Hung House (4 Nguyen Thi Minh Khai)* has decorative shutters and a suspended ancestral altar. For more than 200 years, generations of a single clan have lived in *Tan Ky House (daily 8am–noon, 2–5.30pm | 101 Nguyen Thai Hoc)*. Note the intricate filigree carvings. Another house to include in your five entries is the *Chapel of the Tran Family (daily 7am–6pm | 21 Phan Chu Trinh)*, where there are some fine ivory carvings. *Diep Dong Nguyen House (80 Nguyen Thai Hoc)* was formerly a trading office for Chinese medicines and herbal remedies. *Opening times usually 8am–5pm or 8am–6pm | ⊙ 3–4 hrs for approx. 5 houses/temples*

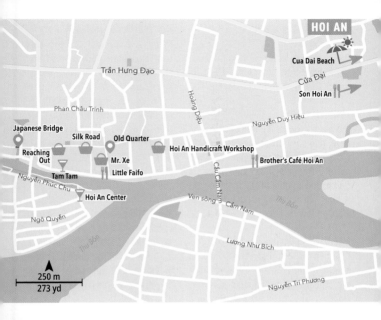

HOI AN

Cua Dai Beach

Trần Hưng Đạo

Cửa Đại

Son Hoi An

Hoàng Diệu

Phan Châu Trinh

Nguyễn Duy Hiệu

Japanese Bridge

Silk Road

Old Quarter

Hoi An Handicraft Workshop

Reaching Out

Mr. Xe

Brother's Café Hoi An

Nguyễn Phúc Chu

Tam Tam

Little Faifo

Cầu Cẩm Nam

Hoi An Center

Ven sông Cẩm Nam

Thu Bồn

Ngō Quyền

Thu Bồn

Lương Như Bích

250 m
273 yd

Nguyễn Trí Phương

EATING & DRINKING

BROTHER'S CAFÉ HOI AN

An idyllic spot by the Thu Bon River. Relax in a colonial villa with a tropical garden, wooden interior and exposed beams, and enjoy good Vietnamese or international cuisine. Well-stocked wine cellar. Book your table for the evening. *27 Phan Boi Chau | tel. 023 53 91 41 50 | £££*

LITTLE FAIFO

In this wonderful Old Quarter restaurant, after a champagne welcome, you dine on one of two levels to the sound of piano music (booking essential for the balcony) and enjoy fine local cuisine. The prawns in ginger and tamarind sauce are tasty, as is the cheesecake. *66 Nguyen Thai Hoc | tel.*

023 53 91 74 44 | littlehoiangroup. com/faifo-restaurant | ££

SON HOI AN

The whole Son family is busy in this kitchen. A rustic and romantic slow-food restaurant among palm trees and rice paddies, serving lovingly plated dishes (mostly Vietnamese food and barbecue) with soft jazz music. *232 Cua Dai | tel. 023 53 86 11 72, 090 5 70 71 44 | ££*

SHOPPING

Hoi An is famed for its bespoke tailoring service (order in good time, preferably with a pattern or a sample) and for its silk, most of which comes from China. One metre of natural silk, 90cm wide, costs around £7.50.

HOI AN HANDICRAFT WORKSHOP

For souvenirs, crafts and daily performances of traditional music (10.15am and 3.15pm). 9 Nguyen Thai Hoc

MR. XE

The place to go for a perfect fit, right on time, and with proper prices. Another well-known and professional, but more expensive shop with excellent goods and quality on the same street is Yaly (No. 47 | yalycouture.com). 71 Nguyen Thai Hoc | tel. 023 53 91 03 88

REACHING OUT

Disabled artisans make and sell some beautiful items in this historic building, including handbags, jewellery, clothing and toys. 131 Tran Phu | reachingoutvietnam.com

SILK ROAD

Good Old Quarter boutique where tailor Thuy magics up blouses, dresses and trousers from £17, depending on material and size. 91 Nguyen Thai Hoc | tel. 090 5 35 71 73 | FB: Silk Road Tailor

ACTIVITIES

BOAT TOURS

Take a paddle boat tour along the Thu Bon River, the largest in the province, and explore the artisan and fishing villages in the vicinity (1-hr tours from approx. £1.70).

COOKERY COURSES 🚩

Many restaurants offer cookery courses, some with a visit to the market included. Among them are Vy's Cooking School (in Morning Glory | 106 Nguyen Thai Hoc | tel. 023 53 91 12 27 | tastevietnam.asia), Brother's Café and Tam Tam, or, including an atmospheric boat tour on the Thu Bon River, Red Bridge Restaurant (Thon 4, Cam Thanh, approx. 4km from the centre | tel. 0235 3 93 32 22 | visit hoian.com). You can chug along the river, see the fishermen at work, and combine the whole thing with excellent Vietnamese dishes. At the end, you'll be presented with a chef's apron.

INSIDER TIP
River trip with cooking

LANTERN-MAKING COURSE 🏮

In Hoi An, you can learn how to make your own paper lanterns, which make lovely souvenirs or Christmas presents – a good exercise in dexterity and patience for young and old. At Huynh Van Ba Lanterns, Mr Huynh, who is over 80 years old, cleverly revitalised this art form many years ago. His idea for a bendable bamboo frame that can be pushed together into different shapes and folded down for your journey home has brought him fame across the nation. Today, his family runs one of the largest lantern businesses in the city. Here, you will get original items and can get involved in the workshop yourself. Courses from approx. £3.40 (depending on the number of participants) | 15A Phan Dinh Phung | tel. 093 5 36 01 97 | denlonghuynhvanba.bizz.vn

The canopied Japanese bridge in Hoi An used to join two residential quarters

BEACHES

The fine-sand 🌿 *Cua Dai Beach* is really just a southern extension of China Beach, just 5km from Hoi An (unfortunately it is getting more and more polluted outside the resorts, depending on the wind and weather). *An Bang Beach* can be found further north, with parasailing, sunbeds, bars and eateries on the beach (some of which are very expensive). People who like to walk on the beach will find that the further north they go, the quieter it is.

NIGHTLIFE

If you fancy an evening stroll, then the *Bach Dang* waterfront is ideal.

HOI AN LUNE CENTER

The wonderful *AO* troupe gets on stage in Hoi An: they are young, modern, captivating, funny and charming. The art and dance performances involve everyday items, such as rice baskets that are thrown into the air, bamboo slides, or round fishing boats that become a trapeze. *Shows from 6pm | admission from approx. £25 | Dong Hiep Park, 1A Nguyen Phuc Chu | luneproduction.com*

INSIDER TIP
Flying rice baskets

TAM TAM

A thousand CDs and good mojitos; sit on the balcony and follow events on the lively street below. *110 Nguyen Thai Hoc | tamtamcafe-hoian.com*

AROUND HOI AN

6 CHAM TOWER
10km west of Hoi An / 30 mins by car or moped

There are plenty of unspoiled beaches in the vicinity, but also secret coves and many places of historical interest to explore, including a *Cham tower* and the remains of Hindu temples. One such brick-built tower can be seen near *Bang An*. On the way there, stop off in *Thanh Ha*, a pottery town. Only a few of the potters there sell direct to the public, and those that do usually make products of good quality. 📖 *G7*

7 TRA QUE VEGETABLE VILLAGE
15km north of Hoi An / 1 hr by bike

A green cycling route: in Tra Que, you can take a wonderful dive into the everyday Vietnamese countryside, and learn something about growing vegetables and the art of cooking as well, for example from the amusing Cook Thanh. A relaxing (foot) massage is the crowning experience of this excursion *(approx. £39 | ⏱ 4–5 hrs).*

If you are cycling here for lunch, don't worry if you're a vegetarian when you see the clouds of smoke and meat, fish and seafood in the woks and on the table grilling station at Thanhs eatery *Kumquat BBQ (mobile 098 9 59 59 23 and tel. 023 53 95 01 23 | kumquathoian.com |*

The lanterns in Hoi An are lit when the day draws to a close

££). There's plenty here for vegetarians, too, with dishes like *morning glory (rau muong xao toi)*, which is one of the tastiest Asian vegetables, from the wok, prepared with lots of garlic. *Cam Kim Island* | *G7*

DA LAT

(G11) **The best way to describe the historical development of** ★ **Da Lat (pop. 200,000) is to highlight the fact that it went from a favourite spot for homesick colonial rulers to a tourist hotspot and popular travel destination for Vietnamese newlyweds.**

Its popularity now is mainly down to the fact that young Vietnamese couples regard lakes – like the famous "Lake of Sighs", plus waterfalls and forests, as the epitome of romance. In spring, when the cherry trees are in full pink blossom, the setting is perfect – the only downside being that it rains frequently here. It was in 1897 that Dr Alexandre Yersin founded a sanatorium in this city, which sits at an altitude of 1,475m. It was another 15 years before the first Europeans settled here. For the upper echelons of colonial society, the smart *Palace Hotel* was the perfect place to spend the hot summer months, and it still is today. Those who could afford it, including the last Vietnamese emperor, Bao Dai, built villas in the pine forests above Lake Xuan Huong.

SIGHTSEEING

SUMMER PALACE (DINH 3) 🛖
A yellow-brown villa with about 26 rooms, built in 1933, recalls the days of Bao Dai, Vietnam's last emperor, who ruled until 1945. The imperial living quarters and many private photos are on display. *Daily 7–11am, 1.30–4pm | admission approx. £0.85 | 2 Le Hong Phong |* ⏱ *30 mins–1 hr*

CHUA THIEN VUONG
The three yellow timber pagodas, built in 1958 by the Chaozhou Chinese community, stand on a hill surrounded by pine forests. Of particular interest here are the three Buddha statues, each around 4m high, which were donated by a British Buddhist from Hong Kong. They are made from gilded sandalwood and each one weighs around 1,400kg. *5km southeast of the city centre, via Khe San street |* ⏱ *30 mins*

EATING & DRINKING

CA PHE TUNG 🏴
A real Vietnamese coffee house. The homemade yoghurt has been a classic dish for decades. It can get busy here and there may be cigarette smoke inside, but this is typical of Vietnam. *6 Hoa Binh | tel. 026 33 82 13 90 | £*

CHU BBQ
In this rustic eatery, which seems a bit like a cave under a corrugated iron roof, you cook your own food at the table. There are tasty ribs, prawns and, if you like, chicken claws. They also

serve great sauces. Vietnamese guests swear by this place. Sometimes you even have to wait for a table. *Pham Ngu Lao | tel. 091 2 01 68 92 | £*

LE RABELAIS
Gourmet restaurant with French-style food, a lake view, liveried waiters and piano music (from 7pm). High tea is served 4–5pm. *Hotel Dalat Palace, 12 Tran Phu | tel. 026 33 82 54 44 | £££*

SPORT & ACTIVITIES

BIKING, TREKKING, FUN SPORTS
The pretty surroundings and the pleasant climate provide just the right conditions for outdoor adventure — cycle tours (approx. £1.70 per day), a climb to the top of *Mount Lang Biang* (with detours to the Lat villages), trekking, rock climbing, abseiling, paragliding and canyoning are just some of the options. Always check the equipment and mountain bikes carefully beforehand. One recommended tour operator is *Phat Tire Ventures (109 Nguyen Van Troi | tel. 092 7 79 89 37 | ptv-vietnam.com).*

MOTORCYCLE TOURS
The new Ho Chi Minh Highway brings you to some of the prettiest stretches of road in the highlands as it approaches the border with Laos, crossing over steep passes and through amazing scenery. A safe bet for tours is *Dalat Easy Riders (day tours approx. £15–£30, three days incl. accommodation and snacks from approx. £50–£60/day | c/o Easy Rider Café | 70 Phan Dinh Phung | dalat-easyrider.com).*

AROUND DA LAT

ⓑ PO KLONG GARAI TOWERS ★
65km southeast from Da Lat / 3 hrs by car
Do you feel like a rendezvous with Shiva? Then, it's time to head for the coast in the former kingdom of the Cham. Cacti surround the four chunky Cham towers, located on National Road 20 to Phan Rang. The best time to visit is September/October, when the Cham celebrate their new year by performing traditional songs and dances at the site.

What is so surprising is the good condition of the buildings — the temples were built in the 13th and 14th centuries under King Simhavarman III. You enter the complex through a beautifully decorated gateway. Adorning the inside of the temple tower is a *mukha lingam*, a stylised phallus symbolising Shiva, who is depicted dancing for his subjects. *Daily 7.30am–6pm | admission approx. £1 | ⓧ 30 mins | ▥ H11*

WATERFALLS
8–130 km from Da Lat / 20 mins– 2½ hrs by train or car
Leaving from the old railway station in Da Lat, approx. 500m east of Lake Xuan Huong, a train runs several times a day *(7.45am–4pm every 2 hrs | travel time 20 mins | minimum 20 passengers)* to the Linh Phuoc Pagoda in the town of *Trai Mat*, around 8km east of Da Lat. From here a 7km

signposted trail leads to the beautiful *Tiger waterfall (Thac Hang Cop, route temporarily closed due to restoration work at the time of writing)*, where the few visitors who come here will be greeted by a huge statue of a tiger (without a head).

The waterfalls and (town) lakes are suffering badly from the high demands of the vast Da Nhim reservoir further west (also called Don Duong). The cascades are most impressive at the end of the rainy period (Nov/Dec), including *Prenn waterfall (by the N20, 10km south of Da Lat)*, the *Lien Khuong waterfall (N20, 30km towards Ho Chi Minh City)*, the *Pongour waterfall (by the N20, 45km towards Ho Chi Minh City)* and the huge *Dambri waterfall* near Bao Loc *(N20, 130km towards Ho Chi Minh City). All waterfalls usually charge admission fees of approx. £1 | ⌘ G11*

BUON MA THUOT

(⌘ G10) **Off the beaten track: ox carts instead of moped chaos and souvenir hunters; waterfalls instead of a concrete jungle. And don't forget that Buon Ma Thuot is nirvana for coffee addicts!**

You can sense that the city (pop. 200,000) grew out of a French military station, which was established here in 1910. Many pretty villas have survived from the times when the French chose the cooler uplands as their summer retreat. At a height of about 500m, Buon Ma Thuot is the provincial capital of Dak Lak and is known for having the best coffee in Vietnam.

An impressive natural spectacle: the Pongour Waterfall near Da Lat

The best beans come from the highlands: coffee harvest in Buon Ma Thuot

SIGHTSEEING

MUSEUM OF ETHNOLOGY

If you are interested in the Ede, Hmong and Muong hill tribes, this museum (also called Dak Lak Museum) will provide you with good information. The gong collection is unique – you could easily miss

INSIDER TIP
Don't miss the gongs!

it because of all the colourful traditional costumes, boats and stuffed wild animals. The centuries-old musical instruments are said to have a magical connection to the gods. You can hear gong music – a captivating, tinny monotone sound – at folklore shows with the *Gong Dance* of the Muong tribe and at all the region's festivals. *Wed–Sun 7–11am, 2–5pm | admission approx. £1 | 182 Nguyen Du/corner of Le Duan | ⏱ 30 mins*

TRUNG NGUYEN COFFEE MUSEUM (COFFEE VILLAGE)

Even tea drinkers will become coffee fans here: more than 10,000 items depicting the global history of coffee is beautifully presented in a lovely wooden longhouse, including shiny polished coffeemakers from the 19th century, antique coffee mills, jugs, pots and boxes. And, of course, there are many small cafés serving the best coffee and selling fresh beans in *Coffee Village*. *Daily 7am–5pm | admission approx. £1 | Le Thanh Tong, 3km from the centre | trungnguyen legend.com | ⏱ 1 hr*

INSIDER TIP
Coffee artefacts

EATING & DRINKING

BON TRIEU

Try the delicious *bon bay mon* — wafer-thin beef in sweet and sour sauces. *33 Hai Ba Trung | tel. 091 3 43 67 72 | ££*

AROUND BUON MA THUOT

9 DRAI SAP FALLS

27km southwest of Buon Ma Thuot / 1 hr by car

Until World War II, the province of Dak Lak was used by the emperor as his hunting grounds – that's no surprise, as there's no other region in Vietnam with such a plentiful supply of game. There is also plenty of water, for example, from the *Drai Sap falls*, rumbling in the heart of a rainforest, especially after heavy rainfall. *G10*

10 LAKE LAK

50km southeast of Buon Ma Thuot / 2 hrs by car

Lake Lak, with its plentiful fish, is an ideal habitat for storks, cranes and ducks. Most tourists are attracted here by rowing and birdwatching. The (in)famous elephant rides across the flat area by the lake and the elephant races ended in 2021. There are plans to open an *Elephant Conservation Center* by 2026, using funds from the Animals Asia Foundation. If you see elephant rides or other elephant activities being offered, MARCO POLO recommends not participating (see p. 20). This also applies to other tourist destinations in this province, such as Ban Don (northwest of Buon Ma Thuot) and other "elephant villages". *G11*

11 YOK DON NATIONAL PARK

50km northwest of Buon Ma Thuot / 2 hrs by car

Those who want to go looking for elephants (and to get photos) can join the guided tours in this large national park with its new *Elephant Conservation Centre*. Tigers are said to also be found in the park, alongside some of the last remaining wild elephants, but the tigers are probably not in the accessible part of the park. The three elephants here that used to be ridden can only be observed in their natural habitat: this has been the case since 2018. They can only be captured by cameras, at least in theory. *Tours from approx. £25 | yokdonnational park.vn | G10*

VILLAGES OF THE EDE & JARAI CEMETERY

25–50km from Buon Ma Thuot / 1–2 hrs by car

In *Buon Tua* (also known as Bon Tur) and *Buon Jang Lanh*, you can get to meet members of the Ede hill tribe (also called the Rhade) in their traditional longhouses and stilt buildings. In these tribes, mothers are the heads of the family. Buon Tua, 25km southwest of Buon Ma Thout, is on the route towards the Drai Sap Falls. Buon Jang Lanh (also called Yang Len), is a kilometre north of Yok Don National Park. There is a cemetery for this hill tribe a good kilometre north of the National Park office, with famous graves of the Jarai people, featuring impressive wooden figures. *G10*

HO CHI MINH CITY & THE SOUTH

INTO THE LAND OF A THOUSAND WATERWAYS

In the Mekong Delta, Vietnam displays its most tropical side: sleepy at first glance, yet still full of power, the brown Mekong flows through rice fields and mangrove forests.

The vital artery of the south, with its nine arms or "nine dragons", ensures that the nation's rice bowls are always full – the Mekong Delta is the main area for rice production in Vietnam.

Ho Chi Minh City is the complete opposite of sleepy: it's exciting and loud, busy and confusing. But once you've mastered the first

Rice is simply part and parcel of Vietnam: working the fields near Phan Thiet

hurdle of the chaotic traffic and managed to cross the street – full of endless, whirring two-wheel vehicles – strolling around Vietnam's skyscraper city is really fun. And some corners still look the same as they did in the 1950s, when author Graham Greene visited.

After seeing the compulsory sights, you need to choose what to do next: relax and sunbathe on the beaches of Nha Trang or Phan Thiet/Mui Ne? Or head for the island of Phu Quoc? All are holiday oases of fine sand, crystal-clear sea and coconut trees.

HO CHI MINH CITY & THE SOUTH

Kompong Chhnang

Kratie

ក្រុងកំពង់ចាម

Lộc Ninh

CAMBODIA

វាជធានីភ្នំពេញ
Phnom Penh

Tân Biên

Chơn Thành

Cao Dai Temple ★   3 Tay Ninh

ក្រុងស្វាយរៀង
Svay Rieng

Cu Chi 2

ក្រុងឌុនកែវ
Takeo

History Museum ★

Ho Chi Minh City
(Saigon) p. 98

ក្រុងកំពត
Kampot

Nui Sam 7   Chau Doc
p. 113

Cao Lãnh

Boat tour of the Mekong Delta ★   1 My Tho

8 Ha Tien

Phu Quoc ★
p. 116

Kiên Lương

Vĩnh Long

Bến Tre

Truong Beach

Rạch Giá

Can Tho
p. 111

6 Cai Rang
Floating Market ★

An Thới

Tiểu Cần

6km, 20 mins

Gulf of

Vĩnh Thuận

Trần Đề

Đông Cao

Thailand

1A

Cà Mau

Bạc Liêu

Vĩnh Châu

Cái Nước   Gành Hào

Con Dao 5

Rạch Gốc

50 km
31.06 mi

HO CHI MINH CITY (SAIGON)

(f E–F12) **Ho Chi Minh City, previously known as Saigon (the name is still used informally), has a population of around nine million people and a zillion whirring motorcycles – it is an Asian boomtown and an exciting journey through time between its colonial buildings, food stalls and modern skyscrapers.**

Vietnam's largest city has successfully retained much of its charm from the French colonial period. Next to colonial remnants you can see the Ho Chi Minh City of today: millions of mopeds and motorcycles, with *cyclos* (three-wheeled bicycle taxis) and pedestrians fighting for space in

WHERE TO START?

Get a moped taxi, *cyclo* or taxi to **Notre Dame Cathedral** (*ᅟ d3*), where you can start your walk. Most of the classic hotels, such as the Continental or the Majestic, are situated on Dong Khoi shopping boulevard (Rue Catinat in colonial days). Carry on past the General Post Office and the Old Opera House as far as the river promenade. Or get a first overview of the city from the **Bitexco Financial Tower** (*ᅟ e4*).

between – the result is generally a chaotic free-for-all that somehow keeps moving. Right in the middle of it all you will find colourful, incense-clouded temples and pagodas, and also markets such as *Binh Tay* in Ho Chi Minh City's fascinating "Chinatown", called ★ *Cho Lon*. Cho Lon ("Big Market") used to be a separate town, where refugees from southern China settled about 300 years ago and started trading, and that is precisely what their descendants still do – on the pavements, in the narrow alleys and in the multistorey market halls.

A ⚑ journey by *cyclo* takes you through the – at times breathtaking – traffic (tip: only book journeys organised through your hotel or travel office). Fancy a nice view? Then head to the 265m-high *Bitexco Financial Tower (daily 9.30am–9.30pm | admission 49th floor observation deck approx. £6.80 | between Ngo Duc Ke and Hai Trieu | bitexcofinancialtower. com | ᅟ e4)* with 68 floors, a shopping centre, a helicopter pad and a café on the 50th floor.

SIGHTSEEING

HÔTEL DE VILLE (CITY HALL)/ WALKING STREET

The *Hôtel de Ville*, Ho Chi Minh City's city hall, is a popular rendezvous spot. Built between 1901 and 1908 in the Vietnamese Baroque or gingerbread style, today it is the seat of the city's People's Committee – with a statue of father of the nation Ho Chi Minh on the square in front. From this location at the northern end of the wide

Ho Chi Minh City from up high: a view of the skyline with the Bitexco Financial Tower

Nguyen Hue avenue, you can take an evening stroll on the pedestrianised street (traffic-free at weekends, otherwise only on the wide central strip) past illuminated fountains, travelling street traders and buskers. Finally, you arrive at a residential house on the right decorated with fairy lights and paper lanterns: the *Café Apartments House (42 Nguyen Hue)* is a hotspot for Vietnamese young people, with its ice cream cafés, sushi bars and small, trendy shops like *Let's Partea* and *Sexy Forever*, stacked like shoe boxes over eight floors. Truly worth a photo. *d3*

OLD OPERA HOUSE/
CITY THEATRE

A sight for sore eyes, not only because of the two angels sitting above the entrance. The building, which dates from the early 20th century, was used post-1956 as an assembly hall for part of the South Vietnamese parliament. In 1975, it was re-opened as a theatre, and renamed Saigon Concert Hall. The *AO Show (6pm or 8.30pm | admission from approx. £25 | luneproduction. com)* is funny and well worth seeing. It features acrobats, bamboo bridges and round basket boats. *Dong Khoi/ corner of Le Loi | e3*

GENERAL POST OFFICE

If you need money, go into a telephone booth – yes, really! The ATMs are in pretty old phone booths here. But first, note the striking features of the main post office, built during the colonial era between 1886 and 1891: the high-level cast-iron ceiling, plentiful glass and old maps. Of course, you may be here for a practical purpose,

HO CHI MINH CITY (SAIGON)

Chua Ngoc Hoang ★

History Museum ★

Indika Saigon

Ao Dai Museum

Carmen Bar

Trung Nguyen Legend
(Nguyen Van Chiem)

General Post Office

Mandarine

Qui Cuisine Mixology

War Remnants Museum

Chua Giac Lam

Reunification Palace

Nha Hang Ngon

Hoa Tuc

Wrap & Roll

Hôtel de Ville

Old Opera House/City Theatre

Water Puppet Theatre

Walking Street

Level 23 Wine Bar

Mekong Quilts

Authentique Home
(Le Thanh Ton)

Bun Bo Hue Dong Ba

Sax 'n' Art Club

Authentique Home
(Mac Thi Buoi)

Cho Lon ★

Ben Thanh Market

Chua Quan Am

Trung Nguyen Legend (Ly Tu Trong)

Chua
Thien
Hau

Shield
Sài Gòn

Hàm Nghi

250 m
273 yd

La Habana

Ho Chi Minh Museum

such as to change money, make enquiries in the tourist information office or use those unusually located ATMs. *Dong Khoi (opposite the cathedral)* | ⏱ *15 mins* | 🕮 *d3*

HISTORY MUSEUM ★

If you want to stroll through Vietnamese history in just one hour, you're in the right place in this pagoda-style colonial building: the country's greatest treasures are displayed here, from the impressive Bronze Age drum from the Dong Son dynasty (Room 2) to the colourful clothes of the emperors and traditional costumes of the hill tribes (Room 15). Don't miss the copy of the thousand-arm goddess Quan

thousand-arm goddess Quan Am (Room 7), whose arms and fingers seem to swirl gracefully through the air. Room 12 contains the Dong Duong bronze Buddha from the early Cham era. The museum also stages *performances by the water puppet theatre* if at least ten interested persons come together *(9am, 10am, 11am, 2pm, 3pm and 4pm | ground floor, Room 11)*. Photography is not permitted in the museum. *Tue–Sun 8–11.30am, 1.30–5pm | admission approx. £1, theatre approx. £1.30 | 2 Nguyen Binh Khiem | baotanglich sutphcm.com.vn | ☉ 1–2 hrs | ▥ e2*

CHUA NGOC HOANG ★ 🐖

Ho Chi Minh City's most important pagoda, where heaven and hell sit alongside each other. Here, the Vietnamese worship Ngoc Hoang, the powerful Jade Emperor of Taoism. The main entrance, flanked by guardian figures, leads first to a Buddhist altar. Only afterwards do you arrive in the main hall with the statue of the Jade Emperor, surrounded by his ministers Bac Dau and Nam Tao, plus four guardians.

The Chief of Hell, Thanh Hoang, dominates the side room to the left of the altar. The small Than Tai, the god of finances dressed all in white, is easy to miss. The Torments of the Ten Hells are shown on wooden panels, but heaven is not far away. The small, incense-filled room on the right attracts many childless couples. Here 12 celestial women clad in precious silk give their blessing for children. *73 Mai Thi Luu, north of the city centre | ☉ 1–2 hrs | ▥ d1*

WAR REMNANTS MUSEUM

You need strong nerves for this exhibition. Documented here in detail are the massacres committed by US forces during the Vietnam War on the Vietnamese population, notably at My Lai, as well as information about the after-effects of chemical agents and dioxins used by the US. The building's courtyard shows captured tanks, helicopters and air defence weapons. If you would prefer to spare your children the images, some of which are disturbing, you can leave them in the ☎ play room on the second floor, where women will look after the little ones. *Daily 7.30am–noon, 1.30–5pm | admission approx. £1.30 | 28 Vo Van Tan/corner of Le Qui Do | warremnants museum.com | ☉ 1–2 hrs | ▥ c3*

CHUA GIAC LAM

From the outside, the Chua Giac Lam is rather unspectacular, but it has experienced a lot: the oldest pagoda in Ho Chi Minh City was built in 1744 and is considered one of the most magnificent in the city. Ten monks live in the building, which reflects Taoist and Confucian influences. The most striking features are the 118 gilded wooden statues, including various portrayals of Buddha, ornate carvings on the altar and on the 98 pillars in the main hall. *118 Lac Long Quan, 3km northwest of Cho Lon | ☉ 30 mins | ▥ 0*

REUNIFICATION PALACE

The Reunification Palace (Independence Palace) stands on the foundations of the Palais Norodom, built in 1868 as the seat of the French governor. In 1962, however, a South Vietnamese pilot mounted an attack on the mansion with the intention of killing the hated South Vietnamese president, Ngo Dinh Diem. The damaged building's replacement, which took four years to build, became known as "South Vietnam's White House". But on 30 April 1975, it was stormed by North Vietnamese tanks. The finest room in the palace is the former audience room for ambassadors (second floor). There is a drinks stall on the roof (fourth floor) and a pleasant garden café called 30/4 outside. *Daily 8am–4.30pm | admission approx. £1.30 | visitors' entrance in Nam Ky Khoi Nghia | dinhdoclap.gov. vn |* ⏱ *1–2 hrs |* ▥ *d3*

CHUA QUAN AM

The Fujian community built this pagoda in 1816, dedicating it to Quan Am, the goddess of mercy. It is regarded as one of the most beautiful in the Cho Lon neighbourhood. On the first main altar you will see Thien Hau, revered as the Holy Mother Celestial Empress and Lady of the Sea, with Thich Ca, the historical term for Buddha, alongside her. The name refers to the figure of Buddha in India, Siddhartha Gautama, who is also known as the Buddha of the Present Moment. Smiling satisfyingly at his side is Di Lac, the Buddha of the Future. In the open courtyard, dressed in white is Quan Am, flanked by General Bao Cong, Thanh Hoang, king of hell, and Than Tai, god of finance. *12 Lao Tu |* ⏱ *30 mins |* ▥ *0*

Taoist and Buddhist deities are honoured in the Chua Quan Am pagoda

CHUA THIEN HAU

Legend has it that Thien Hau, the patron saint of fishermen and mariners, can travel everywhere by riding the oceans on a mat or sitting astride the clouds. The pagoda was built in the early 19th century by the Cantonese community to honour the goddess. Considered to be the finest pagoda in the Cho Lon neighbourhood, particularly admired for its magnificent ceilings adorned with colourful ceramic figures, among them a number of miniature demons. *710 Nguyen Trai/corner of Trieu Quang Phuc, centre of Cho Lon | ⏱ 30 mins | ⅢⅢ 0*

HO CHI MINH MUSEUM 🏛

The Nha Rong or "Dragon House", built in 1863 at the point where the Ben Nghe canal joins the Saigon river, is where in 1911, a young communist named Ho Chi Minh, otherwise known as Ba, was hired as a kitchen boy for the *Admiral Latouche Tréville* passenger steamer. Recalled in this interesting museum are this and other periods in the life of the great revolutionary. Do climb to the second floor to see the pop-art posters of Ho Chi Minh, which are a popular souvenir. *Tue–Sun 7.30–11.30am, 1.30–5pm | admission approx. £1 | 1 Nguyen Tat Thanh | ⏱ 30 mins–1 hr | ⅢⅢ e4*

INSIDER TIP
Pop-art posters

AO DAI MUSEUM

See Vietnamese fashion items from the past. The museum shows how Vietnamese people (including noblemen) dressed 300 years ago. It exhibits 500 *ao dais* (Vietnamese women's national dress), richly adorned with dragons, as well as practical farmer's dresses in a hip style with bright colours or in a propaganda style in bright red with a yellow star. You can also try out the look: take selfies in a complete outfit, including a headdress. In the marvellously idyllic park with recreations of ancient pagodas and bridges over lotus ponds, planted with paddy fields, palms and bamboo trees, you can take a lively cultural journey through time *(approx. £1.70)*. At the weekend, there are dance shows, which attract a lot of people. *Tue–Sun 8.30am–5.30pm | admission approx. £3.40 | 30 Long Thuan, Long Phuoc, east side of the city, approx. 1½ hrs from the centre (car/bus no. 88) | FB: baotangao daivietnam | ⏱ 1–2 hrs | ⅢⅢ 0*

INSIDER TIP
Try on traditional clothes

EATING & DRINKING

Always follow your nose, the billows of smoke lead the way: some of Ho Chi Minh City's best seafood eateries line up outside on Vinh Khanh street one after the other, among them *Oc Oanh (no. 534 | £ | ⅢⅢ e5)*. The large barbecue and hot pot eateries in Trung Son a bit further south are a little more expensive *(£–££ | ⅢⅢ 0)*, each with 300 seats under a tin roof – and all the charm of a railway station

INSIDER TIP
Street food – good catch!

hall. Whether you choose goat or pork, gigantic barbecued prawns or squid, or scallops with roasted peanuts *(so diep nuong mo hanh)*, you will eat your fill for £8.50.

BUN BO HUE DONG BA

This soup restaurant serves just one dish: *bun bo hue*, the noodle soup from the imperial city of Hue – with beef strips, bean sprouts, banana blossoms and morning glory (water spinach), plus a chilli or fish sauce. *110 Nguyen Du, near Ben Thanh market | FB | £ | ⌂ d4*

LA HABANA

Tapas and mojitos, sangria and salsa, cigars and paella — a popular bar-restaurant with the most distinctive Spanish-Cuban ambience imaginable in this socialist brotherly state. You can get a Wiener schnitzel here, too. *152 Le Lai | tel. 028 39 25 98 38 | FB: La Habana.SG | ££ | ⌂ c4*

HOA TUC

Some people regard this slightly hidden restaurant as one of the best in Vietnam. What is certain: not only is the atmosphere good here (it's in an old opium factory and adjoining courtyard), but the food is also beautifully presented, a feast for the eyes as well as the tastebuds. And the service is fast. To try preparing the food so you can enjoy it back home, reserve a place on a cookery course! *74/7 Hai Ba Trung, opposite Park Hyatt Hotel | tel. 028 38 25 16 76 | hoatuc.com | ££–£££ | ⌂ e3*

MANDARINE

Dine with traditional Vietnamese music in the background. This is a sophisticated restaurant with sophisticated flavours and appropriately high prices – duck in orange sauce, seafood and fish at its finest, vegetarian dishes and menus from £14. Popular with tour groups. *11A Ngo Van Nam | tel. 090 8 87 00 99 | mandarine.com.vn | £££ | ⌂ e3*

NHA HANG NGON

Always a full house here for authentic Vietnamese cuisine. Sit outdoors or inside in the two-storey building. Be sure to try the delicious *goi bo bop thau*, a spicy beef salad with banana and slices of star fruit. *160 Pasteur Ben Nghe | tel. 028 38 27 71 31 | FB: Nhahang.QuanAnNgon | ££ | ⌂ d3*

TRUNG NGUYEN LEGEND

The Trung Nguyen coffee house chain is known for its relaxed atmosphere. This branch is a chilled oasis over several floors. It serves Vietnamese-style drip coffee, as well as cappuccinos and iced coffees. There are also small dishes and cakes in candy colours. *7 Nguyen Van Chiem, near the cathedral | ⌂ d3; branch: 219 Ly Tu Trong, near Hindu Temple and Ben Thanh market | ⌂ d4 | £*

WRAP & ROLL

A thousand and one variations on the spring roll in a modern snack bar chain. Whether with prawns or Hue style – it's always delicious. As well as breakfast, the menu lists salads, soups and desserts, fish and vegetarian

An alternative to Rembrandt copies: propaganda posters make a trendy souvenir

dishes, and hot pots in the evening. *62 Hai Ba Trung* | FB: *wraprollVN* | £ | ⬜ *e3*

SHOPPING

The boulevards in District 1 invite you on a shopping spree for silk clothing and lacquerware, especially in the streets of *Dong Khoi* (⬜ *d–e3*), which is rather expensive, Hai Ba Trung, Le Loi and Nguyen Van Troi (for galleries). You'll find Armani and Gucci, a great food market, plus games rooms for youngsters in the ⬆ *Vincom Center (70 Le Thanh Ton,* ⬜ *e3)*. Antiques and Buddhas in all shapes and sizes can be found in *Le Cong Kieu* (⬜ *d4),* for example from the *Ngoc Bich family (no. 64).*

Cheap and cheerful imitations, DVDs and T-shirts are available in the *Saigon Square 1* department store (*Nam Ky Khoi Nghia, near Ben Thanh market,* ⬜ *d3)* and *Saigon Square 3 (Hai Ba Trung,* ⬜ *d2)*.

The chaotic *Binh Tay Market* in Cho Lon, the *An Dong Market (An Duong Vuong,* ⬜ *b5)*, Ho Chi Minh City's largest market, and the *Nguyen Dinh Chieu Market (1 Le Tu Tai,* ⬜ *0)*, an outdoor market with everything from clothes to gold to teas, are reasonably priced.

The streets around the backpackers' row *Pham Ngu Lao* (⬜ *c–d4),* such as the "Painting Streets" Tran Phu and Bui Vien, are where you can find fake masterpieces. In and around *Le Duan* (⬜ *d2–3)* you can wander around the quiet little streets, past cafés and stands with books and souvenirs. If you are looking for new shoes, you are likely to find something in Ly Chinh Thang (District 3). Some shops also make custom shoes.

AUTHENTIQUE HOME

Pretty decor, and artistic and practical items for the living room back home: wonderful hand-painted cups and vases, wall carpets, embroidered cushions, bags and so on – not exactly cheap, but these are not mass-produced merchandise. Pottery and ceramic workshops are also offered. There are two branches. *113 Le Thanh Ton | ⊞ d3; 71/1 Mac Thi Buoi | ⊞ e3 | authentiquehome.com*

BEN THANH MARKET

This huge market has around 1,500 stands. Be preopared that some 90 per cent of the "branded items" are fakes, from watches to trainers, whisky to Picasso paintings. But you can also find great souvenirs near the western entrance. If you want to find a bargain, come in the late afternoon. Otherwise, you will have to negotiate down to half the original price, if not a third. Be calm but friendly and you will get the discount. Unfortunately, there are lots of pick-pockets around. In the evening, there is a night-time market with food stalls. *Le Loi and Le Lai | ⊞ d4*

**INSIDER TIP
In time for a bargain**

MEKONG QUILTS

You can purchase nice souvenirs here, made from rattan, paper-mâché or bamboo (there are even bamboo bike frames). The hats, scarves, bags, textiles, clothing and quilts are made by under-privileged women, who earn four times more here than their wages elsewhere. *85 Pasteur St, Ben Nghe district | mekongquilts.com | ⊞ d3*

ACTIVITIES

Hop on a moped with *XO Tours (tel. 093 3 08 3727 | xotours.vn)*. Female drivers in *ao dai* dress will collect you and take you, for example, on their *XO Foodie Tour*. The company provides full accident insurance. There is a new travel option from *Saigon Sidecar Adventure (tel. 093 2 19 99 91 | sidecaradventurevietnam.com)*: sit in the sidecar of old Russian military motorbike to go through the city for a few hours.

Trails of Indochina *(6D Ngo Thoi Nhiem | tel. 028 35 35 04 55 | trails ofindochina.com)* offers half- or full-day tours with unusual cultural experiences, such as investigating Vietnam's contemporary art scene.

WELLNESS

LA MAISON L'APOTHIQUAIRE SPA

One of the best day spas in town pampers its guests in an old villa (pick-up service). *Daily 9am–8pm | 64a Truong Dinh | tel. 028 39 32 51 81 | lapothiquaire.vn | ⊞ d3*

NIGHTLIFE

CARMEN BAR

Loud, cool … and filled with smoke! It's an absolutely fun and brilliant location, with unbeatable atmosphere and diversity. Live bands, predominantly Latino and flamenco, play in this dimly lit setting. Cocktails, beer,

**INSIDER TIP
Vietnam, Spanish-style!**

wine and whisky are served. It's packed to the rafters at weekends. *8 Ly Tu Trong* | 🗺 *e3*

INDIKA SAIGON

It can get very busy in Indika. It's not difficult to make new friends in this hip restaurant-bar at the open mic events and over board games. They serve wood-fired pizza, lasagna, bagels, bowls and burgers *(££)*. You can sit in the beautiful, rustic inner courtyard or inside in the dimly lit interior, listening to the rock music.

So why not come here at night for a drink and to see the sparkling 180-degree view? *Sheraton Tower, 88 Dong Khoi* | *short.travel/vie10* | 🗺 *d3*

QUI CUISINE MIXOLOGY

You have to spoil yourself sometimes: whatever your choice – well-chilled wine, champagne or cocktails – the bartenders know what they're doing here. The food is also tempting – and fairly pricey. *22 Le Thanh Ton* | *quilounge.com* | 🗺 *e2*

Pedestrians, cyclists, mopeds: chaotic traffic in Ho Chi Ming City

43 Nguyen Van Giai (at the end of the lane) | *FB* | 🗺 *d1*

LEVEL 23 WINE BAR

Have a dignified time on the 23rd floor of the Sheraton: quiet sounds, courteous waiting staff, knowledgeable bar staff and a good wine menu.

SAX 'N' ART CLUB

Small and friendly jazz club run by saxophonist Tran Manh Tuan. Large screen and jazz videos to watch while sipping your drink, until the live bands get started from 9pm. Happy Hour *5–8pm. 28 Le Loi* | *FB: saxnart* | 🗺 *d3*

SHIELD SÀI GÒN

If your ears are still ringing three days after a night out in Ho Chi Minh City, you were probably in the popular bar called Shield in the middle of the backpackers' quarter around Pham Ngu Lao. It has a rare mix of music for Vietnam: rap and hip hop. Enjoy the vibe and the cocktails! *19 Do Quang Dao | FB: ShieldSaigon | ⊞ c4*

WATER PUPPET THEATRE 👤

Dragons swoop energetically over the water and spray people in the first row, astounding young and old alike. The *Rong Vang Golden Dragon Water Puppet Theatre (⊞ d3)* is a fine example of the genre, with 200 seats. Performances last around 50 minutes *(Thu and Fri, 6.30pm | admission approx. £10 | 55b Nguyen Thi Minh Khai | tel. 028 39 30 21 96 | golden dragonwaterpuppet.vn)*. Water puppet theatre also takes place during the day in the *History Museum* (see p. 100).

AROUND HO CHI MINH CITY

1 MY THO

70km south of Ho Chi Minh City / 2 hrs by car or bus

The first busy spot on the road out to the Mekong Delta is the provincial capital of My Tho (pop. 180,000). This is a good place to start a ★ *boat tour of the Mekong Delta*. Countless companies shout out about their offers on the riverside road *30 Thang 4*, not far from the tourist information office. The long-tail boats, with their rattling engines and long propeller shafts, often have to squeeze through narrow channels on their way past tiny temples, busy markets, coconut groves and banana plantations. Possible destinations include the *floating market of Cai Be*, the islands of *Con Phung* (Coconut Monk island) or *Thoi Son*. Be prepared to negotiate a price. Don't pay more than £8.50 per boat for a two-hour tour. *⊞ F12*

2 CU CHI TUNNELS ⚑

60km west of Ho Chi Minh City / 1½ hrs by car or bus

The moment you arrive, you will be reminded of the horrors of war. At the entrance to the Cu Chi Tunnels in the village of *Ben Dinh*, you will see the gun of a rusty tank taking aim, and beside it a military helicopter. The visitors' entrance leads into a 50m-long restored section of a cool and damp tunnel, which, despite widening, is still quite narrow. These underground routes, formerly controlled by the Viet Cong, once extended for 250km, covering an area of about 400km². They were equipped with canteens, hospitals and rest rooms – all up to 10m below ground. The tunnels were so narrow that only the slender Vietnamese could squeeze through. Women were often brought underground to give birth in safety; mother and child were then able to stay there for weeks. The first tunnels were dug in 1948 during the battle against the

A mix of cathedral and mosque: the Cao Dai Temple in Tay Ninh

French. An open-air museum and a war memorial remind us of grim wartime events. A shooting range provides a macabre place to while away the time for visitors who want to continue playing war despite all the wartime atrocities described here. *Daily 7am–5.30pm | admission approx. £3.40 | on the N22 to Tay Ninh | ⏲ 2 hrs | ▢ F12*

3 TAY NINH
95km west of Ho Chi Minh City / 2 hrs by car or bus

The home of the Cao Dai religion: Tay Ninh (pop. 42,000) is the capital of the province of the same name and, since 1927, the centre of this faith. Many are inclined to dismiss Caodaiism as a rather contradictory fusion of various beliefs, but the town is definitely worth a visit, if only to admire the extraordinary, colourful architecture of the ★ *Cao Dai Temple*. It can be found in the village of Long Hoa, about 4km east of the city centre, on a spacious concourse (the "Holy See"), on which at times up to 100,000 faithful followers lived.

The temple itself is a mixture of a twin-tower cathedral, a pagoda with round tower and a mosque with a domed roof. The deep blue sky on the roof, with stars made from mirror glass, the pillars entwined with dragons, the octagonal altar and the globe are striking features inside. The prayer ceremony is held four times a day – at 6am, noon, 6pm and midnight. Tourists may watch from the upstairs balcony. Ceremonies in the morning can get very crowded, so it is advisable to attend the evening or midnight prayer session.

The volcanic cone of the 1,000m *Nui Ba Den* (Mountain of the Black Woman), 15km northeast of the city centre, provides an outstanding view. It was once a holy shrine for the Khmer and is still a place of pilgrimage. 𝌆 *E12*

◢ CAT TIEN NATIONAL PARK
160km northeast of Ho Chi Minh City / 4 hrs by car

If you go exploring here, with a little luck, you will see – and hear – the endangered yellow-cheeked gibbons: they are famous for their early-morning duet choruses, which are guaranteed to give you goose bumps!

The park is also one of the last refuges of the Indochinese tiger; plus, there are also clouded leopards and the gaur, a wild cattle species – though you won't usually see them when you tour the park because they hide in the jungle (if they haven't fallen prey to poachers). You are more likely to see crocodiles, scorpions and leeches. Over 350 bird species fly around the park, including colourful kingfishers and hornbills.

A visit to the British-run *Primate Center* is also worthwhile, as is a stop at the *reintroduction project for Asian black bears and wild cats (go-east.org)* and the "Gibbon Trek" *(from 4.40am).* You can go on an exploratory tour with a guide (book at least four days in advance), for which a charge of about £17 per day is made, or dash around

Will you see (and hear) the gibbons in Cat Tien National Park?

on the trails on a hired bike (check it beforehand). Huge trees extend their roots onto the path, which is great for photos. Basic overnight accommodation (*£, electricity only until 6pm, bring a torch!*) is available at the park entrance. *Admission approx. £2.50 | information from the National Park Service (office in Than Phu at the bus stop, 24km from the park | tel. 025 13 66 92 28 | namcat tien.org) | 𝄚 F11*

5 CON DAO
300km south of Ho Chi Minh City, towards Con Son / 1 hr by plane

The Con Dao archipelago, which consists of 16 islands in the South China Sea, is slowly but surely becoming a holiday destination. The mountainous main island of *Con Son* is rather infamous because the French began interning prisoners here in 1862, later followed by the South Vietnamese and Americans, who kept thousands of political prisoners and opponents of the regime here. Today, both of the prisons – *Phu Hai* and *Phu Thuong* – have been turned into museums. The archipelago is a national park and conservation area that is popular among divers. Over 1,300 species of ocean dwellers inhabit the wonderful coral reefs, including turtles, dolphins, whales and sea cows (dugong). The best time to visit is between November and February. Flights depart Ho Chi Minh City daily for Con Son; night ferries depart from Vung Tau (*𝄚 F12*). *𝄚 F14*

CAN THO

(*𝄚 E13*) **Long-tail boats, so called because of their outboard motors with elongated propellers that sweep through the water like a whisk, shuttle continually back and forth along the countless canals and meandering waterways.**

The boat drivers navigate their wooden craft along often very narrow channels, as some homes and stilt houses are far from the main river. If you would like to explore the Mekong Delta off the beaten track, then you would be well advised to find accommodation in one of the hotels in this city populated by 800,000 people, which forms the political, commercial and cultural centre of the delta, and explore from there.

SIGHTSEEING

MUNIRANGSYARAM TEMPLE

A centre for Cambodian Buddhism: around one million Cambodians from the neighbouring country live in the Mekong Delta, which the Vietnamese occupied in the 18th century. The Buddhist Khmer can still be identified by their traditional *kramas* (checked scarves) and sarong-type skirts. You enter the temple, built in 1946, through an impressive portal in Angkor Wat style. The house of worship, with its stepped roof, is the meeting place of the local Khmer community. The first floor of the main building contains a 1.5m-high statue of the Buddha Sakyamuni under a

Shops for early risers: stalls at the Cai Rang Floating Market

Bodhi tree. *Daily approx. 8–11.30am, 2–5pm | admission free | 36 Hoa Binh |* ⏱ *20 mins*

DINH BINH THUY "ANCIENT HOUSE"

Enter and travel through time: the house, built in 1870, is a true jewel. It's not surprising that it's often used as a filming location. For example, Jean-Jacques Annaud filmed scenes here for his adaptation of Marguerite Duras's novel, *The Lover*, here. The house exhibits newspaper clippings, photos and notes as a witness to those times. The premises has impressive tiled roofs, curved stairs, carvings and valuable antiques. If the great-grand-child of the original builder is here, you will hear some details about the colonial history of the premises (in French) and be shown some of the exhibited treasures, such as the

beautiful washbasin made of porcelain. If you come on a national holiday, you can enjoy a sample of 700-year-old Vietnamese opera *(hat boi)* by the *Phuong An Ensemble* and, if you ask on site, you can take a course in singing, music and dancing. The opera performers wear splendid costumes and masks, or they wear a lot of makeup. A four-day temple festival with sacrificial rituals and opera takes place every year at the end of May/beginning of June. There's also a small café. *Daily 8am–noon, 2–6pm | 142–144 Bui Huu Nghia | admission approx. £0.40 |* ⏱ *30 mins*

EATING & DRINKING

SAO HOM

A popular restaurant in the old market hall at a nice spot by the river, which is nearly always full. Huge selection of seafood, Chinese, Indian and Vietnamese classics such as spring rolls and hot pots, some western (French) dishes and an excellent ice-cream menu. There are also a number of inexpensive food stalls on the banks of the river. *50 Hai Ba Trung, Ninh Khieu pier on the promenade near the night market | tel. 029 23 81 56 16 | FB: saohomrestaurant | ££*

NIGHTLIFE

How about a trip on the Hau Giang river? Noisy three- or four-storey *restaurant and disco vessels*, adorned with strings of flashing lights, leave daily at 6pm and 8pm from Ninh Kieu Park promenade. Perhaps — like the Vietnamese — you will enjoy this garish nightlife. It's a bit of Las Vegas in the Mekong Delta. Or, if you prefer something quieter, you can enjoy an evening stroll on the enormous new *Ninh Kieu pedestrian bridge*, with its bright nighttime illuminations.

AROUND CAN THO

6 CAI RANG FLOATING MARKET ★ ⚑
7km southwest of Can Tho / 20 mins by boat or car
The most attractive of the so-called "floating markets" in the Mekong Delta: every morning, countless rowing boats and long-tail boats heavily laden with melons and pineapples,

cucumbers and soup saucepans, and more, congregate near the Da Sau bridge. You could spend hours watching the lively market scene. It's best to watch the whole spectacle from the water: hire a boat from the centre of Can Tho near the market *(approx. £8.50 for 2 hrs)*. Get up early: it all gets going at sunrise and goes on until about 8am; by 9am activity is starting to tail off. ⏱ *1 hr | ▥ E13*

CHAU DOC

(▥ D12) **Everyday life in Chau Doc, a city with a population of 200,000 near the Cambodian border, still proceeds at a leisurely pace.**

The city is a melting pot of cultures: Vietnamese live here alongside Chinese, Khmer and Cham. Long-tail boats chug sedately along the Hau Giang river, children jump into the water from the decks of houseboats, which float on empty oil drums. Many houseboats have nets slung beneath them, in which hundreds of thousands of catfish are farmed. The catch is then transported to small fish-processing factories in the city, where they are dissected, deep frozen and exported all over the world. The city is also an important centre for the Vietnamese silk industry.

SIGHTSEEING

CHAU GIANG
Cross the river either by ferry or private boat to the Cham village of Chau

Giang. The Cham weavers are keen to tell visitors about their centuries-old weaving skills and also to sell, at very affordable prices, their delicately patterned wraparound skirts. A short walk through the village will take you to the *Chau Giang mosque* (take your shoes off, and women should cover their head and ask permission to enter), hard to miss given its dome and tower. There's a great view over the town and the river from the tower. *Ferries leave from Chau Chiang jetty in Chau Doc about every 5–15 mins |* ⏱ *1 hr*

EATING & DRINKING

There are lots of snack stalls and mini eateries on Bach Dang around the market hall – just point to what you want and take a seat on the plastic stools.

BASSAC

Even if you don't treat yourself to anything else, you should indulge in a French meal on the romantic riverside veranda of the Victoria Hotel (à la carte or buffet). *1 Le Loi | tel. 028 62 90 97 20 | victoriahotels.asia | ££–£££*

MEKONG

Quiet, friendly and still reasonably priced: stop for a bite to eat with the three female cooks directly opposite the fancy Victoria Hotel. Sit on the plastic seats and look through the menu for your feast. *41 D Le Loi | tel. 029 6 32 86 27 32 81 | ££*

ACTIVITIES

Speedboats run every day over the border to Cambodia (and back): Express boats from *Blue Cruiser (approx. $55 plus $34 for the Cambodia visa | FB: bluecruiservn)* go directly to Phnom Penh. The *Hang Chau Express Boats ($32 | book at mommup96719@gmail.com)* are a little more expensive. The *Victoria Sprite (tel. 18 00 59 99 55 | victoria hotels.asia)* is exclusive, expensive and only open to guests at Victoria Hotel. *Duration of journey approx. 4–5 hrs each way.*

INSIDER TIP
Fast boat to Cambodia

AROUND CHAU DOC

🔟 NUI SAM

5km south of Chau Doc / 20 mins by car

The panoramic view from this 230m mini-mountain takes in the surrounding landscape of hills and rice fields, right into the region close to the Cambodian border. At sunset an air of mystery surrounds the many small temples and pagodas. Taoists, followers of Cao Dai, Christians, even Buddhists and Muslims, flock to Nui Sam in their thousands for the midnight festivities at New Year and also the annual Via Ba festival (April/May). ⏱ *2 hrs |* 🗺 *D12*

8 HA TIEN

80km southwest of Chau Doc /
2 hrs by car

The area around Ha Tien is known as the "Ha Long Bay of the south". The town itself, with its population of 40,000, is surrounded by hills and lies in a bay in the Gulf of Thailand. Since the border to nearby Cambodia some 10km away was opened, more and more tourists have been island- and beach-hopping from Vietnam along the Cambodian coast to Thailand, which has benefitted Ha Tien too. In the early 18th century, the Chinese Mac family pacified what was then a small settlement here, and built it up into a fiefdom. One survivor from that era is the *Phao Dai* fortress, with a view over the bay, and the small *Dong Ho* or "East Lake", which is squeezed between two granite cones known as the *Ngu Ho* and the *To Chau*. Elaborately decorated with dragon carvings, phoenixes, lion heads and guardian statues are the family tombs of the Mac dynasty, *Lang Mac Cuu (Nui Lang | 3km northwest of the town centre, accessible via the Mac Tu Hoang)*. Worshipped in the pretty pagoda, *Chua Tam Bao (Mac Thien Tich)*, built between 1730–50, are the goddess of mercy, Quan Am, and the Jade Emperor. By the market and riverbank lies the highly recommended Xuan Thanh restaurant *(corner of Ben Tran Hau/Tham Tuong Sanh | tel. 029 73 85 21 97 | £)*. ☐ D12

Firmly rooted: a Mac dynasty tomb

PHU QUOC

(□ C–D 12–13) **Spend your holiday where pepper grows! ⭐ Phu Quoc, Vietnam's largest island, is close to the Cambodian border and is changing at breakneck speed.**

The plots for countless luxury resorts have already been earmarked (unfortunately many of them are currently building sites). Awaiting exploration, mainly on the south coast, are some 40km of beaches fringed with coconut palms against a jungle backdrop. A luxury casino (Corona) and a 27-hole golf course (at the Vinpearl Hotel) have opened, and three other golf courses are planned, as well as a huge cruise ship terminal. A cable car stretching 8km across the sea connects with the neighbouring island of Hon Thom – with concrete pillars protruding skywards, ten times higher than the coconut palms. Phu Quoc (pop. 180,000), with its capital city *Duong Dong*, is said to be Vietnam's answer to Phuket, with a targeted five million holidaymakers visiting every year, some staying in rapidly constructed resorts with their own marinas and high-rise apartment complexes. The main attractions are the gigantic *VinWonders theme park and VinPearl safari park,* with fairytale castle, zebras and giraffes. Here, Las Vegas flair mingles with a wildlife and African ambience. In the winter season, there are daily flights to Phu Quoc from Ho Chi Minh City, Can Tho and Rach Gia, as well as several speed boats *(approx. £8.50, including the* red boats of Phu Quoc Express), departing from Ha Tien and Rach Gia.

SIGHTSEEING

PHU QUOC NATIONAL PARK
Phu Quoc means "99 mountains". However, the mountains in the north of the national park, which rise to a height of 603m, are mostly still part of a restricted military zone. On the rough track by the east and north coast, tall trees provide welcome shade, while the crickets in the rainforest sound like a whistling kettle. If you make a tour around the national park and arrive near the fishing village of *Ganh Dau*, you can see the coast of Cambodia and its Seh Island just 4km away.

EATING & DRINKING

EDEN
Three-storey venue by the southern section of Truong beach. From breakfast eggs to beach bar, from billiards to disco dancing — all needs are met from early morning until late at night. *118 Tran Hung Dao (Beach Road) | Duong Dong | tel. 029 73 98 55 98 | edenresort.com.vn | ££*

KOZE BARBECUE
Large BBQ restaurant that always has smoke-free areas. Beef ribs sizzle away at the table in a sweet and spicy Korean-style marinade, along with pork belly slices, making your mouth water. You can watch the chefs preparing food in the open kitchen. *129 Trang Hung Dao | tel. 091 1 11 68 86 | £–££*

NEMO

It's pleasant sitting in the garden of the open-air restaurant on Beach Road – seafood is presented outside on ice

INSIDER TIP
Delicious seafood dish!

before being barbecued. Try the prawns in tamarind sauce – and order them again and again! *Tran Hung Dao, Cua Lap | tel. 093 9 54 45 51 | ££*

SPORT & ACTIVITIES

DIVING

The fishermen in An Thoi or pleasure boats belonging to the hotels (from Truong Beach) will take you to the offshore islands, such as *Hon Doi Moi* or "Turtle Island" in the north – the best snorkelling is from *Vung Bau* beach – and to the tiny *An Thoi archipelago* in the south, noted for its fine coral reefs in crystal clear water. With visibility up to 15m from October to April, the diving waters here rank among the best in Vietnam. During the diving season, *Rainbow Divers (Duong Dong, at the start of Tran Hung Dao/Beach Road | tel. 091 3 40 09 64| divevietnam.com)* organise PADI courses.

HIKING

You can walk to a number of small waterfalls and springs to the southeast of Duong Dong, for example to the *Suoi Tranh* spring, and also to caves and pepper plantations. The best time for excursions to the islands is during the dry season in winter.

BEACHES

The *Truong Beach (Long Beach)* on the west coast, south of Duong Dong, is a 20km-long, golden yellow, palmfringed sandy strip, which extends as

Sun, sand, jungle – a palm beach on Vietnam's largest island, Phu Quoc

A red landscape: walking through the Red Sand Canyon

far as the fishing harbour at *An Thoi* on the southern tip of the island. It's almost the only place in Vietnam where you can see the sun set from the beach.

The beautifully curved *Ong Lang Beach* (north of Duong Dong) has several kilometres of sandy bays broken up by rocky headlands. In the far south, near An Thoi, lie the snow-white powder sand and palm trees of *Sao Beach*. However, it is at times so crowded with people, deckchairs and plastic water slides that you can barely see it.

NIGHTLIFE

DINH CAU NIGHT MARKET

An endless feast: at the *Dinh Cau Night Market* in the island's capital of Duong Dong, you can get fresh seafood and fish (hot pots, king prawns, cuttlefish, and so on) for £1.50–£2.50. Simply go from stand to stand trying things. *Daily 5–10pm | Vo Thi Sau*

PHAN THIET

(▢ *G12*) **Hawaii can wait – because slalom and freeriders know what "side-onshore winds" mean: the perfect wave!**

But the 20km stretch of palm trees and sand on the Mui Ne Peninsula near the port city of Phan Thiet (pop. 200,000) is not only the country's most popular beach destination for surfers. Around 200 hotels stretch along the 16km-long coast road, some of which is like a boulevard. The long, sun-drenched coastline – with its varied landscape ranging from Sahara-style dunes to rainforests — attracts investors and tourists alike. However, subject to the season, wind and weather, the beach can get badly eroded and polluted. By the way, Phan Thiet is famous in Vietnam for its fish sauce. Despite the masses of beachgoers, you will still see fishermen attending to their boats, nets and baskets on the beach – in some places it's very narrow.

SIGHTSEEING

MUI NE ★

It's all beach: unpack your bikini or bathing shorts, stretch out and relax, and watch the kite- and windsurfers on ✈ *Mui Ne Beach*. Or try climbing on the surfboard yourself. Whatever your choice, Mui Ne offers plenty of variety. The small town in the centre of the Mui Ne Peninsula has a lively harbour and some small fish sauce factories.

Gleaming brightly at the end of the peninsula are the celebrated reddish-orange to yellowy-white dunes of *Bao Trang*. You can get to the top in a jeep or a quad bike, or you can walk – but not barefoot. As early as 9am, the sand is red hot!

PO SHANU TOWERS

Near Mui Ne Beach, on the *Ngoc Lam hill,* stands Vietnam's southernmost Cham shrine. Dedicated to Queen Po Shanu, the three small Po Shanu towers, dating from the eighth century, are less ornate than the famous towers of Po Nagar and Po Klong Garai. A beautiful panoramic view extends from here along the coast and over the town of Phan Thiet. *Admission approx. £0.50* | ⏱ *15 mins*

EATING & DRINKING

RUNG FOREST RESTAURANT

Large, rustic jungle-like restaurant with terracing on to the street. Mainly Vietnamese cuisine, but also pasta, wines and cocktails. Folkloric-themed performances take place in the evening. *67 Nguyen Dinh Chieu* | tel. *098 3 99 87 49* | ££

SPORT & ACTIVITIES

HIKING

One popular walk (approx. 1 hr) starts near the village of *Ham Tien* and follows a creek through the dunes and past the bright red rock walls of the small *Red Sand Canyon* as far as the cascading source of the *Suoi Tien* ("Fairy Springs").

WINDSURFING & KITE SURFING

Every February, hundreds of water sports enthusiasts meet up in Mui Ne for the *Fun Cup*. As Phan Thiet and Mui Ne are in what is considered to be a low rainfall region, the resorts attract an international band of windsurfers throughout almost the entire year. The best times for surfing are September/October to December, for kite surfing November to March/April. *windsurf-vietnam.com*

GOING OUT

JIBE'S

Where the surfers meet up in the evening – in the middle of the beach. *90 Nguyen Dinh Chieu, km13* | *windsurf-vietnam.com*

MIA MUI NE

Popular lifestyle club with the excellent Sandals Restaurant *(£££),* which serves fusion food and has an up-market beach bar serving great cocktails. *24 Nguyen Dinh Chieu, Ham Tien* | *sailingclubmuine.com*

Po Nagar Temple is one of the few buildings preserved from early Cham culture

AROUND PHAN THIET

9 TA CU

30km southwest of Phan Thiet / 1 hr by car or moped

On the 694m-high Ta Cu (also known as Ta Ku) in the nature reserve of the same name is what is probably the tallest Buddha statue in Vietnam. The Sakyamuni Buddha measures a total of 49m from the tips of his toes to the top of his enlightened head. To reach the statue involves either a two-hour hike through the woods, or – more comfortably – a ten-minute cable-car ride. Pilgrims and visitors are drawn to the peace and quiet here. At the top

they are welcomed to the over 150-year-old *Linh Son Truong Tho* monastery *(daily 7am–5pm | admission including cable car approx. £8.50 | near Ham Thuan Nam | ⏱ 1–4 hrs | 🗺 G12*

NHA TRANG

(🗺 H11) **The rapidly developing coastal town of ⭐ Nha Trang has grown into a busy tourist centre with an ever-changing skyline.**

A wild fusion of Nice and Ibiza, with bonfire parties and fire shows, go go girls, shishas and pool bars – you will likely be greeted by Russian music here. In a broad bay on the South

China Sea, the city (pop. 450,000) is bordered to the north by a small mountain range, including Son mountain. Offshore are a number of green islands, which look the perfect place for dreamy afternoons lounging beneath palm trees. The Tran Phu waterfront seems to go on forever, following the beach for more than 5km. It ends in the south at the fishing harbour of Cau Da.

SIGHTSEEING

PO NAGAR

The Po Nagar Cham temple on a hill in the north of town has become a symbol for Nha Trang. Consisting of four towers, it was probably built between the ninth and 13th centuries. It is dedicated to Po Ino Nagar, the goddess who watches over the city and is an incarnation of the wife of Shiva (Durga, also known as Parvati). From the pagoda complex, there is a fine view over the harbour and its brightly painted fishing boats. *Daily 6am–6pm | admission approx. £1 |* ⏱ *30 mins*

LONG SON PAGODA

Built in honour of Kim Than Phat To, the White Buddha, who sits in a highly visible position to its rear. Some 152 stone steps lead up from Long Son, past a huge reclining Buddha. The pagoda itself was built in the late 19th century. Look out for the brightly coloured dragons wrapped around the pillars either side of the main altar. *Thai Nguyen, 500m west of the train station |* ⏱ *1 hr*

EATING & DRINKING

LAC CANH 🐷

You'll be happy you got a table here. Just follow the clouds of smoke: this eaterie – admittedly with all the charm of a railway station – serves mountains of seafood (from £1.70), chicken and beef from the barbecue. Everything is cooked at the table in the tastiest marinades, and served with vegetables. *Tiger Beer* flows like a river, the coals glow and the place is abuzz – always loud, full and authentic. The menu is also available in English. *44 Nguyen Binh Khiem | tel. 025 83 82 13 91 | £*

INSIDER TIP
Best of BBQ

NHA TRANG VIEW

Don't be put off by the price – here, it's the kilos that count! It's best to work up a good appetite or arrive in a family group at this romantic seafood restaurant and café. It's situated off the "party mile" just before the bridge over the bay and offers a fantastic (nighttime) panorama of the coastal metropolis. Choose your seafood fresh from the seawater tanks. The grilled scallops *(so diep nuong mo hanh)* are a real delight, garnished with spring onions and chopped peanuts. *Lau Ong Tu, north end of Tran Phu | tel. 090 5 12 06 68 | nhatrangview.com.vn | £–££*

INSIDER TIP
Scallops with a garnish

SHOPPING

LONG THANH GALLERY

Long Thanh is one of the best photographers in Vietnam. You can buy posters in this small gallery depicting everyday comings and goings that always tell a story – atmospheric, black-and-white art with some surprising perspectives, for example with the camera under a fisherman's net, as if the photographer himself is being caught. *Daily 9am–4.30pm | 126 Hoang Van Thu | longthanhart.com*

INSIDER TIP
Photographs of the everyday

SPORT & ACTIVITIES

ISLAND TOURS & CABLE CAR

Boat tours to the offshore islands are very popular. Don't be too thrifty when booking one, and ask other travellers about their experiences with the various travel agencies, such as *T & T Travel (102 Hung Vuong | tel. 097 4 25 47 80 | FB: T&T Travel Nha Trang)*.

A *cable car* crosses the sea to *Hon Tre (daily 8am–10pm | approx. £25, including the admission to the VinWonders amusement park)*.

You may find affordable private guides for other excursions by moped or bicycle here: *toursbylocals.com/Nha-Trang-Tour-Guides*

… and now relax: on Nha Trang Beach

DIVING

Rainbow Divers (Rainbow Bar, 90a Hung Vuong | tel. 090 5 07 19 36 and 092 25 28 87 32 | divevietnam. com) is the leading diving operator in Vietnam and also offers courses in Nha Trang.

BEACH

The 6km-long, broad Nha Trang Beach is lined almost entirely with coconut palms. Hire a lounger and enjoy a relaxing day.

NIGHTLIFE

Ibiza-style beach parties are popular events. Someone somewhere lights a bonfire, then house music or a gentle lounge sound emanates from speakers, and nobody goes to bed before sunrise.

LA LOUISIANE BREWHOUSE & RESTAURANT

Live music and beer tastings. 29 Tran Phu Beach | louisianebrewhouse. com.vn

SAILING CLUB – SANDALS RESTAURANT

From 10pm onwards this dimly lit garden and beach restaurant is also a popular disco club. It's crowded, loud and hot (with a camp fire). International crossover dishes are served (£££), along with lots of cocktails. 72–74 Tran Phu | sailingclub nhatrang.com

AROUND NHA TRANG

⑩ THAP BA HOT SPRINGS

10km north of Nha Trang / 10 mins by car or taxi

Let's start with the mud bath: wellness and relaxation can be found in Vietnam in tubs of mud (37–38° celsius), as well as hot-water springs (40° celsius), Jacuzzis and waterfalls. If you want to, you can follow it all with a massage. For young visitors, there's a 👯 children's pool. If the public area of the mud baths is too busy for you (especially at weekends), there are mud bath tubs for families and couples (from approx. £12) and (overpriced) VIP areas and premium packages. Daily 7am–7.30pm | adults approx. £5, children from approx. £2 | 15 Ngoc Son (Ngoc Hiep) | tel. 025 83 83 53 35 | tambunthapba.vn | ⏱ 2–3 hrs | 🗺 H11

⑪ DOC LET BEACH 🌴

50km north of Nha Trang / 2 hrs by car

If you crave tranquillity and solitude, then this idyllic beach on the Hon Khoi Peninsula (fork off near Ninh Hoa) is the place to go. The kilometre-long, flat beach is empty on weekdays and has many restaurants and guesthouses to offer. 🗺 H10

DICOVERY TOURS

Want to get under the skin of this country? Then our discovery tours are the ideal guide – they provide advice on which sights to visit, tips on where to stop for that perfect holiday snap, a choice of the best places to eat and drink, and suggestions for fun activities.

❶ OUT AND ABOUT IN THE MEKONG DELTA

➤ Cycle through orchards in the delta
➤ Chug up to floating markets on a boat
➤ Take a jungle canoe tour through green sunken forests

📍 Ho Chi Minh City

🏁 Tra Su Reserve

→ around 450km

🚗 3 days, driving time (without stops) 6 hours

ℹ️ Cost: approx. £300 for two people.
In the rainy season (April/May–Oct), the roads are full of potholes, and are sometimes closed because of flooding. Cars and bicycles can be rented from several companies, for example *Focus Asia (focus.asia); Sinhbalo Adventure Travel (sinhbalo.com)* is tried and tested.

Among the water buffalo: sometimes they block the roads

FRUIT PLANTATIONS AND FLOATING MARKETS

The tour begins in ❶ Ho Chi Minh City ➤ p. 98. *Take the congested highway 1A to* ❷ My Tho ➤ p. 108, a city that lives on trade and the fact that millions of people in Ho Chi Minh City need to be supplied daily with rice, pineapples, bananas and oranges – all products of the Mekong Delta. Whatever does not make its way to the metropolis is sold by traders in the bustling market quarter of My Tho. Experience the magic of the Mekong on a *boat tour leaving from the city. On the* ❸ Ben Tre *peninsula disembark and hop on a bicycle. Cycle along the narrow paths under the coconut trees and through orchards before taking the boat back to My Tho.*

The terrain *of the next stage of the route towards Vinh Long* is entirely flat. Women wearing typical straw hats can be seen working the rice paddies everywhere. ❹ Cai Be is home to an impressive market *(daily, approx. 5am–5pm)* typical of the Mekong region: ⚑ buyers and sellers make their way along the Tien Giang, the "Nine Dragons", as the Mekong's tributaries are known, on flat-bottomed boats with long wooden rudders. If you have had enough of the delta for the day, check in at the luxurious Victoria Can Tho Resort *(victoriahotels.asia)*

DAY 1

❶ Ho Chi Minh City

75km · 1hr

❷ My Tho

18km · 1hr 10mins

❸ Ben Tre

44km · 45mins

❹ Cai Be

69 km · 1hr

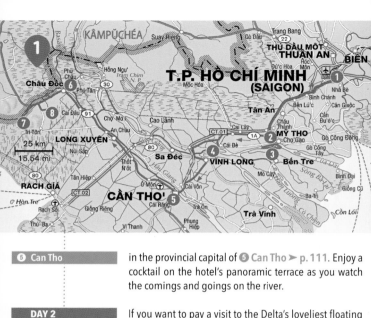

5 Can Tho

in the provincial capital of **5** Can Tho ➤ p. 111. Enjoy a cocktail on the hotel's panoramic terrace as you watch the comings and goings on the river.

DAY 2

If you want to pay a visit to the Delta's loveliest floating market, the Cai Rang Floating Market ➤ p. 113, you should try to get there early, between 6am and 7am, which is the busiest time of day.

DISCOVERIES IN THE LAND OF THE KHMER

130km 2hrs

6 Chau Doc

Afterwards, continue driving along the N91 to **6** Chau Doc ➤ p. 113. The floating houses of the fish breeders are the town's trademark. An evening trip up the mountain Nui Sam, located 5km to the south, is an enjoyable way to end the day. Also make sure to stroll through the town, with its ethnic mix of Muslim Cham, Khmer and Vietnamese.

DAY 3

58km 1hr 10mins

7 Ba Chuc

Take a half-day excursion to the Khmer village of **7** Ba Chuc with its traditional temple and shocking exhibit in the "Bone Pagoda", a modern monument resembling a UFO in which the skulls of war victims are stacked behind glass.

34km 45mins

8 Tra Su Reserve

Then *go off to discover some of the region's unspoilt nature in the magical* **8** Tra Su Reserve.

Jungle birdlife

INSIDER TIP

You can go bird-watching aboard a canoe in its sunken forest, where thousands of storks, herons, cormorants and other waterfowl breed. If you want to enjoy some peace and quiet on your boat, avoid coming here at the weekend.

❷ FROM HANOI TO THE WONDERS OF HA LONG BAY

➤ Ahoy: set sail for a cruise in a dream-like bay
➤ Caves, lagoons, intriguing rocks
➤ Climbing in Cat Ba: a bird's eye view of Ha Long Bay

📍 Hanoi	🏁 Ha Long City
➡ around 200km	🚗 3 days, driving time (without stops) 3 hours

ℹ Cost: approx. £315 for two people. Hire car/boat trip, for example, with *Tam Travel* (*tamtravel.com.vn*) and *Asiatica Travel* (*asiatica.com*).

DAY 1
❶ Hanoi

RED RIVER AND COLOURFUL SUGAR CAKES
The best place to start is in ❶ Hanoi ➤ p. 42 at the old post office near Lake Hoan Kiem ➤ p. 44 From here, it's easy to reach the *Chuong Dong Bridge, which crosses the Red River as you make your way out of town. Continue on Highway 1 through the bustling district of Gia Lam and then take the N5.*

59km   1hr

Soon, the first green rice paddies come into view. The reddish-brown silt, which the river carries for more than 1,800km, has made this region quite fertile. After the heavy summer rains, some of the area floods, necessitating the construction of new dykes that you cannot miss. *After 59km, you will come to the provincial capital* ❷ Hai Duong. Now it's time for a

❷ Hai Duong

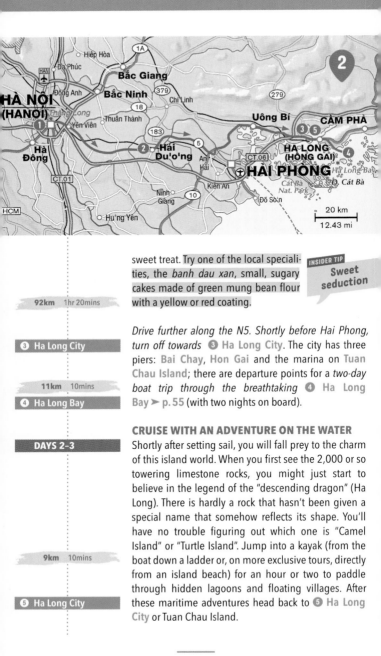

sweet treat. Try one of the local speciali-ties, the *banh dau xan*, small, sugary cakes made of green mung bean flour with a yellow or red coating.

INSIDER TIP
Sweet seduction

92km 1hr 20mins

Drive further along the N5. Shortly before Hai Phong, turn off towards ❸ **Ha Long City**. The city has three piers: **Bai Chay**, **Hon Gai** and the marina on **Tuan Chau Island**; there are departure points for a *two-day boat trip through the breathtaking* ❹ **Ha Long Bay** ➤ p. 55 *(with two nights on board)*.

❸ **Ha Long City**

11km 10mins

❹ **Ha Long Bay**

CRUISE WITH AN ADVENTURE ON THE WATER

DAYS 2-3

Shortly after setting sail, you will fall prey to the charm of this island world. When you first see the 2,000 or so towering limestone rocks, you might just start to believe in the legend of the "descending dragon" (Ha Long). There is hardly a rock that hasn't been given a special name that somehow reflects its shape. You'll have no trouble figuring out which one is "Camel Island" or "Turtle Island". Jump into a kayak (from the boat down a ladder or, on more exclusive tours, directly from an island beach) for an hour or two to paddle through hidden lagoons and floating villages. After these maritime adventures head back to ❺ **Ha Long City** or Tuan Chau Island.

9km 10mins

❺ **Ha Long City**

CLIMBING WITH A VIEW
Ha Long's rocks are not only a fairy-tale land, they are also popular with climbers. The national park island of Cat Ba ➤ p. 58, along with the adjacent Lan Ha Bay ➤ p. 35, are true paradise for rock climbers!

❸ MANGROVES, MOUNTAINS AND A COASTAL DRIVE

➤ Hunting – with a camera and long socks – in the forest
➤ The Da Lat mountains: perfect for honeymooners
➤ Have fun swimming off the coast

📍 Can Gio   🏁 Nha Trang

→ around 700km   🚗 5 days, driving time (without stops) 11 hours

ℹ Cost: approx. £580 for two people.
What to pack: torch, anti-leech socks, mosquito repellent (there is malaria in the area).
Recommended time to travel: Nov/Dec–March/April (dry season).
Car rental from, for example, *VN Rent a car (vnrentacar.com)*
❸ **Cat Tien National Park**: register at least 4 days in advance and book a guide *(namcattien.org)*!

DISCOVER THE MANGROVES FROM A KAYAK
The tour begins 55 kilometres southeast of Ho Chi Minh City in the alluvial sand of ❶ Can Gio (800 km²), an island formed by the Saigon river, which is famous for its mangrove forest. Although largely destroyed by the Agent Orange defoliant used by the US military in the Vietnam War, the forest, with its trees atop buttress roots, has once again become a haven for many species of fish, reptiles (such as monitor lizards) and birds. It is even home to a macaque colony. Try to get an early start, around 8am if you can, for a two-hour tandem kayak tour in order to avoid the busloads of tourists.

DAYS 1–2

❶ Can Gio

TO THE HIGHLANDS AND THE NATIONAL PARK

Drive towards Ho Chi Minh City and turn onto the N1 heading northeast. After the industrial town of Bien Hoa, at km69 in Dau Giay, follow the N20 as it branches off towards the mountains, passing rubber plantations and fruit trees. Many fishermen live on houseboats and in floating villages on the ❷ Tri An reservoir. *After about 70 km, near Phu Thanh, a track leads off* to ❸ Cat Tien National Park ➤ p. 110.

INSIDER TIP
Jungle hike

On arrival, you can hike for 5km, taking around three hours, on a jungle trail to Crocodile Lake. For a faster journey, you can rent a bicycle. Keep your eyes peeled for the different kinds of birds and, with a bit of luck, even some gibbons and colobine monkeys. You can spend the night at Crocodile Lake, for example, in the Green Bamboo Lodge *(Rooms and tents | FB: Green Bamboo Lodge Enjoy Nature)* or outside the national park in the stylish yet rustic Forest Floor Lodge *(forestfloorlodges.com)*. Explore the national park in more depth the next day – this time accompanied by a guide.

135km 2 ¼hrs	
❷ **Tri An reservoir**	
45km 40mins	
❸ **Cat Tien National Park**	

WATERFALLS AND HONEYMOONING

Drive along the bumpy road back towards the N20, crossing through Ma Da Gui (four-wheel drive is a must in the rainy season!). The route slowly winds up to a height of 1,500m, where dense jungle surrounds the pass. You can see a few picturesque temple shrines and waterfalls by the wayside. *You will come to the plateau near the small town of* ❹ Bao Loc, which is an ideal place to tour tea factories or silkworm farms. The best time to see the waterfalls ➤ p.90 is at the end of the rainy season (Nov/Dec), including ❺ Dambri waterfall *(near Bao Loc)* and the ❻ Pongour waterfall *(near Duc Trong, 48km south of Da Lat).* Poster-clad walls and greenhouses herald your arrival in the mountain town of ❼ Da Lat ➤ p. 89, a favourite destination among Vietnamese honeymooners.

DOWN TO THE WHITE BEACHES BY THE SEA

Leave Da Lat heading eastwards towards Phan Rang on the serpentine N20, and turn onto the N27 towards the coast. You can't miss the ❽ Da Nhi reservoir and the huge hydropower plant. The fascinating ❾ Ngoan Muc Pass, from which you can see the coast about 60km away if the weather is good, *winds around 1,000m down to the lowlands,* where palm trees and cacti abound. *A few kilometres before arriving at the coastal town of Phan Rang,* you will see the Cham temple Po Klong Garai ➤ p. 90 on top of a hill and, around 15km south of Phan Rang, Po Rome. *Depart Phan Rang via the Coastal Highway 702 to the north.* The road runs past fishing bays, white beaches and green hills. Luxury hotels with spectacular settings await along the way, such as the ❿ Amanoi Resort *(aman.com)* in the amazingly beautiful Vinh Hy Bay. The seaside restaurants built on stilts here offer plenty of refreshment.

Coastal Highway 702 runs further north to Bing Tien near the harbour of Cam Ranh, which served as a US Navy base from 1964–73. *Drive a bit further north on the N1 to the seaside resort of* ⓫ Nha Trang ➤ p. 120. Spend a relaxing day at the beach to end this tour.

DAY 3

60km   1hr

❹ **Bao Loc**

18km   20mins

❺ **Dambri waterfall**

93km   1½hrs

❻ **Pongour waterfall**

48km   40mins

❼ **Da Lat**

DAY 4

37km   45mins

❽ **Da Nhi reservoir**

5 km   5 Min.

❾ **Ngoan Muc Pass**

129km   1½hrs

❿ **Amanoi Resort**

DAY 5

99 km   1½hrs

⓫ **Nha Trang**

GOOD TO KNOW

HOLIDAY BASICS

ARRIVAL

GETTING THERE

Vietnam Airlines fly direct from London to Ho Chi Minh City and Hanoi daily for around £700 return; the flight time is around 12 hours. A number of airlines, including Vietnam Airlines, Qatar Airways and American Airlines, fly from New York, Los Angeles and other US cities from around US$800 return. When booking onward flights within Vietnam or to neighbouring countries, the Vietnamese national carrier often grants a 50 per cent discount. *vietnam airlines.com*

ON ARRIVAL

UK citizens do not need a visa for tourist (or business) travel to Vietnam, if you are staying for 45 days or fewer. For trips over 45 days, an e-visa can be obtained *(evisa.xuatnhapcanh.gov.vn)*,

 + 6 hours ahead in summer

Vietnam time is 7 hours ahead of Greenwich Mean Time, 6 hours ahead in summer. It is 15 hours ahead of Standard Pacific Time and 12 hours ahead of Eastern Standard Time.

which allows a 90-day stay and multiple entries; other types of visa are available from the Vietnamese Embassy or via a Vietnamese travel agent. US citizens require a visa (obtainable as an e-visa, valid for up to 90 days with multiple entries) for tourist or business travel. All travellers' passports must have an expiry date of at least six months after arrival in Vietnam, and at least two blank pages.

Citizens of the US and other

People use sticks to help them transport items across the Mui Ne sand dunes

 Adapter Type A

Mains voltage is usually 220V. Pack a universal adapter.

GETTING AROUND

DOMESTIC FLIGHTS

Vietnam Airlines operate daily flights linking all the major cities. A Ho Chi Minh City to Hanoi return ticket (two-hour flight) costs from £135, much less with low-cost airlines *Viet Jet Air (vietjetair.com)* and *Jetstar Pacific Vietnam (jetstar.com/vn/en/home)*. You must book well in advance during the Tet Festival.

countries that normally require a visa can travel visa-free forup to 30 days on the island of Phu Quoc, for example by directly flying from Bangkok with *Bangkok Airways (bangkokair.com)*. However, if flying internationally to Hanoi or Ho Chi Minh City with a stop at Phu Quoc, US citizens, and those from other nations normally requiring visas, must not leave the transit area. If you want to visit other destinations after Phu Quoc, you will need a visa, which you must apply for in advance.

When you arrive in Vietnam, you must fill in an entry form and customs declaration, a duplicate of which must be submitted when you leave.

HIRE CARS & MOPED TOURS

A hire car with a driver is the time-honoured way to take an individual, independent tour. Ask for details at a travel agency *(incl. driver/petrol from approx. £38/day, flat rate per kilometre, plus £25/day flat-rate fee for a guide.)*. Tourists need an international driving permit to drive a car; riding a moped with a more than 50cc engine is officially not permitted (and dangerous). Beware: Vietnam is one of the countries in Asia with the most deaths on the roads and there are no efficient emergency services, such as you find in western countries. Tourists are allowed to be passengers for moped tours with more powerful vehicles with professionals, for example with the company *Easy Rider (Da Lat | dalateasyrider.com)* or *Xo Tours (Ho Chi Minh City | xotours.vn)*. You must wear a helmet in Vietnam. If you are planning a tour and want to travel by moped taxi often, you should bring a good helmet from home with you, because Vietnam does not have the best-quality, safest helmets.

International car rental companies: *Avis (avis.com.vn), VN Rent a Car (vnrentacar.com)*

MEKONG TOURS

Mekong Eyes Cruise (Can Tho | tel. 076 17 66 49 76 | mekongeyes.com) organise boat tours on a converted rice barge with 30 double rooms. Another good tour operator is *Sinh Balo Adventure Travel (283/20 Pham Ngu Lao | Ho Chi Minh City | tel. 028 38 37 67 66 | sinhbalo.com | 2 days for 2 pers approx. £205/pers)*. If you want luxury travel, then investigate *Pandaw Ships (pandawcom)*, which run between Ho Chi Minh City/My Tho and Angkor in Cambodia.

PUBLIC TRANSPORT

Trains run every day between Hanoi and Ho Chi Minh City. A journey on the *Reunification Express* between north and south runs five times a day there and back. The journey takes 32–38 hours. If you like comfort, travel with a first-class *Soft Sleeper* ticket, which you should book in advance.

Travelling by public overland bus is not advisable, as there have been many serious accidents. If you want to travel on a tourist bus, ask in the traveller cafés about *Open Tours*. The buses, with reclining seats, are comfortable (Hanoi to Hue costs approx. £13). *Mai Linh Express Bus (tel. 028 39 39 39 39 | mailinh.vn)* and *Hoang Long (tel. 022 53 92 09 20 | hoang longasia.com)* are reliable bus companies. Online tickets for plane/train/bus, also payable by credit card, are available from travel agents such as *baolau. vn, 12go.asia/en* and *dsvn.vn*.

Hanoi has an underground metro (*tickets from £0.25, day tickets from £1.10*). On Cat Linh Line 2, trains run

FESTIVALS & EVENTS
ALL YEAR ROUND

Most traditional festivals follow the Chinese lunar calendar. As the lunar month is only 29 or 30 days and the lunar year has 354 or 355 days, every three years an extra month is added between the third and fourth lunar month.

JANUARY/FEBRUARY

Tet Nguyen Dan: The Vietnamese New Year is the most important family event. Celebrations can go on for a week. Flights get booked up very quickly *(1st day of 1st month of the lunar calendar; usually end of Jan/Feb. Next dates 29 Jan 2025, 17 Feb 2026)*

APRIL

Thanh Minh: Celebration of ancestors at graveyards *(5th day of 3rd month; usually in April)*

Huong Tich Fest: Spring pilgrimages to the temples of Huong Tich Son *(15th day of 3rd month; usually in April)*

MAY

Phat Dan: Buddha's birthday *(8th day of the 4th month; usually in May)*

MAY/JUNE

Tet Doan Ngo: Midsummer festival *(5th day of the 5th month; usually end of May/June)*

AUGUST/SEPTEMBER

Trung Nguyen: Celebration of ancestors with offerings at altars in the home and at temples *(15th day of 7th month; usually Aug/Sept)*

SEPTEMBER/OCTOBER

Le Hoi Choi Trau: water buffaloes sacrificed at harvest time *(regional: Do Son at Hai Phong, 8/9th day of 8th month; usually Sept)*

⭐ **Trung Thu:** Vietnamese Valentine's Day and and a mid-autumn festival, which also celebrates children, with lantern processions at night under a full moon *(15th day of 8th month; usually Sept/Oct)*

between northern-central Hanoi and the deep southwest (outside the Old Quarter and West Lake) via Ha Dong. The Van Mieu Line 3 (in construction at the time of writing), running from east to west, will terminate at the train station. In Ho Chi Minh City, a metro system is planned to be open by the end of 2024.

TAXIS & CYCLOS

In Hanoi and Ho Chi Minh City, many taxis have meters *(approx. £0.48/km, basic tariff approx. £0.48)*. Unfortunately, fraud is common. If the figure on the meter appears to be rising rapidly and the driver keeps beeping their horn, ask them to stop, pay the stated sum and get out. If you want a taxi from your hotel, order an official taxi or only use official, reputable companies. In Ho Chi Minh City, *Vinasun (tel. 028 38 27 27 27)* and *Vinataxi (tel. 028 38 11 11 11)* are reliable and *Mai Linh (nationwide tel. 10 55)* is available throughout Vietnam. *Uber* is also a quick, safe way of getting around Vietnam, even in the small cities. *Grab* is an Asian version of Uber. Here, though, you generally have the choice to pay by cash or card.

Cyclos, or cycle-hauled rickshaws, are common in Vietnam; it is normal to negotiate a price in advance *(approx. £1.70–£3.50/hr)*; in Ho Chi Minh City/1st district and Hanoi/Old Quarter prices can rise steeply, possibly up to around £7 per hour, depending on your negotiation skills. Moped taxis are also popular (always wear a helmet). In many cities, such as Can Tho, there are motorised *cyclo* taxis – a

moped in front of a two-seater carriage *(approx. £0.45/km)*. As it is difficult for tourists to figure out how the rather sparse public bus service operates (only available in Ho Chi Minh City and Hanoi), the taxi in all its different manifestations is the main way of getting around for visitors.

EMERGENCIES

UK EMBASSY HANOI

Central Building, 4th floor, 31 Hai Ba Trung, Hanoi | tel. 04 39 36 05 00 | ukinvietnam.fco.gov.uk/en

UK CONSULATE HO CHI MINH CITY

25 Le Duan Street, District 1, Ho Chi Minh City | tel. 028 38 25 13 80

US EMBASSY HANOI

7 Lang Ha Street, Hanoi | tel. 024 38 50 50 00

US CONSULATE HO CHI MINH CITY

4 Le Duan Blvd. Dist. 1, Ho Chi Minh City | tel. 028 35 20 42 00 | hochiminh. usconsulate.gov

ESSENTIALS

BANKS, MONEY & CURRENCY

The Vietnamese *dong* (VND) is the local currency. The notes range in value from 10,000 to 500,000 VND. Beware: the 20,000 and 500,000 notes look very similar. There are ATM machines in all towns, which charge low fees (usable by Visa, MasterCard, and Maestro in large tourist cities). You can change US dollars and pounds without any problem. Large hotels, tourist restaurants, travel agencies and airline offices accept credit cards *(up to 4 per cent handling fee)*. It's a good idea to use the licensed, privately run change bureaux de change *(usually open 7am–10pm, for example in Dong Khoi street or at Ho Chi Minh City's General Post Office)* or those in larger jewellery shops. As the theft of smaller sums of money from rooms, luggage, even room safes, is common, if possible leave your money in the safe at reception and ask for a receipt.

CUSTOMS

Visitors may import 1.5 litres of high-percentage alcohol or 2 litres of wine and 200 cigarettes or 100 cigars or 500g of tobacco into Vietnam duty-free. To export antiques, you will need to obtain an export certificate.

DONATING MONEY

If you want to help the poor, donate to one of the charitable organisations that cares for street children and people with disabilities, such as *Saigon Children (saigonchildren.com), Reaching Out (reachingoutvietnam. com)* in Hoi An or the *Hoa Sua School (hoasuaschool.edu.vn)* in Hanoi.

HEALTH

No vaccinations are required for Vietnam, unless you have arrived from a yellow-fever zone. However, protection against polio, tetanus,

HOW MUCH DOES IT COST?	
Coffee	£0.45 for a cup in a café
Noodle soup	£0.85–£1.70 in a restaurant
Taxi journey	approx. £0.50 per kilometre
Beer	from £0.20 for a draught beer in a restaurant
Clothing	from £25 For an ao dai dress
Massage	from £5 to £7 on the beach

diphtheria, hepatitis A/B and typhus is recommended. A stand-by medication is advisable in malaria regions (high risk of malaria in the regions bordering Cambodia, otherwise low to no risk). To avoid diarrhoea, do not drink tap water or even use it to clean your teeth. Do not eat unpeeled fruit or salad, unless you are dining in an international hotel. The same advice applies to ice cream. Because of the risk of cholera in north Vietnam (mainly Hanoi and Ninh Binh), it is probably better to avoid it altogether. A well-tolerated oral vaccine against cholera is available at hospitals specialising in tropical medicine. Dengue hemorrhagic fever and chikungunya has been reported mainly in the south of Vietnam (primarily in the Mekong Delta region, but also in Ho Chi Minh City). The virus is transmitted by a mosquito, which is active during the daytime. The best form of prevention is to wear bright, long-sleeved clothing and use a mosquito repellent. There is no vaccine. For up-to-date information, contact your doctor's surgery or consult the website of a hospital specialising in tropical medicine. A health insurance policy is essential. Make sure cover includes medical evacuation costs.

INTERNET ACCESS & WIFI
WiFi is available for free almost everywhere (except for some luxury hotels): hotels and cafés, airports and even some bus stations and (overnight) buses (*Mai Linh and Phuong Trang/ Futa*, very slow and it pays to have a pre-paid card). There are Internet cafés all over the country where you can Skype or Zoom, even in isolated mountain regions. The government blocks social networks every now and then, but you can often circumvent this problem by using a proxy server (look into one ahead of time).

OPENING TIMES AND ADMISSION
Do not expect opening times to be adhered to exactly. Many museums are closed on Monday or at least from 11.30am to 1.30pm. Unless otherwise stated, admission is free.

PUBLIC HOLIDAYS

1 Jan	Tet Duong Lich (Christian New Year)
3 Feb	Founding of the Vietnamese Communist Party (1930)
30 April	Liberation Day (fall of Saigon to North Vietnamese forces in 1975)
1 May	Labour Day
2 Sept	National Day (Declaration of Independence, 1945)

TELEPHONES & MOBILES
Calling abroad from your hotel costs between £0.50–£1/US$0.80/$1.30. It is often cheaper to use an IDD phone card, obtainable from post offices and some telephone kiosks *(up to approx. £0.18/min)*. Cheapest of all are the internet cafés (for Skype or Zoom). Calls are free, but connections are often poor. Turning off the webcam can help to improve sound quality. Also use WhatsApp for free calls over the internet.

Viettel, Vietnamobile are cheap mobile phone providers; *Vinaphone* and *Mobifone* are more expensive ones. You can use a Vietnamese SIM/ pre-paid data card, for example *Happy Tourist*, sold by SIM card street traders or small shops, which then validate them. Then it only costs a small amount to call home; the price varies according to the data volume up to 6GB *(approx. £0.15/US$0.25/min)*. Text messages cost approx. £0.08/ US$0.13 to Europe and North America. You will need an unlock code and will be allocated a new telephone number (you'll probably prefer to buy a new mobile phone for £8–£12/US$13–$17 in Vietnam). As there are many expensive telephone numbers (such as the easy to remember 4 00 40 04 00), when you buy, make sure you ask for a "cheap" number. If you are using a British or American provider, extra hidden charges are added by the Vietnamese companies to incoming calls, in some cases up to £0.80/ US$ 1.20 per minute. For information on roaming agreements see *gsmworld. com.*

The country code for the UK is 0044, USA 001 and Vietnam 0084. Then dial the local area code without the zero.

TIPS

Feel free to tip good service, but in the better-class restaurants and hotels, the bill often already includes a service charge. Tips are not expected at the food stalls. In hotels, you can tip about 20,000 VND (approx. £1) per day. On group trips, a tip will usually be collected at the end for the driver and the tour guide, approx. 150,000 VND per person per day for both together (approx. £4.20).

WEATHER & WHEN TO GO

If you go to the south, the best time is between December and March, when the temperatures are bearable and there is little rainfall. In April/May, it can be oppressively sultry ahead of the rainy season (June to December). The months of June to November bring heavy storms and occasionally floods to central Vietnam and the Mekong Delta region.

The further north you go, the greater the differences between summer and winter, and you can tell there are four distinct seasons. Sub-tropical summers from April onwards can be hot and humid, while from December to February the temperatures on the central/north coast can fall well below 20°C. In addition, long periods of drizzle can spoil the enjoyment of travel.

WEATHER IN SAIGON

■ High season
■ Low season

	JAN	FEB	MARCH	APRIL	MAY	JUNE	JULY	AUG	SEPT	OCT	NOV	DEC
Daytime temperature												
	32°	33°	34°	35°	33°	32°	31°	31°	31°	31°	31°	31°
Night-time temperature												
	21°	22°	23°	24°	24°	24°	24°	24°	23°	23°	23°	22°
Sunshine hours/day	6	8	7	7	5	5	5	5	5	5	5	6
Rainy days/month	2	1	2	4	16	21	23	21	21	20	11	7
Water temperature in °C	24	25	25	28	28	28	28	28	28	27	27	25

☀ Sunshine hours/day   🐾 Rainy days/month   ≋ Water temperature in °C

USEFUL PHRASES IN VIETNAMESE

SMALL TALK

yes(depending on region)	có; ừ; dạ	go; öh; dja
no/maybe	không/có lẽ	chong/go lä
Please	Xin; Làm o 'n	sin; lahm ön
Thank you	Cám ỏn	gahm ön
Good morning/day/evening/night/Hello	Xin chào!	sin djau
Goodbye/Bye	Chào tạm biệt!	djau dahm bi-eh´
My name is …	Tên tôi là …	dönn teula
What is your name?	Anh/Chi tên gí?	an/chi dönn sji
Sorry/Excuse me	Tôi xin lỗi!	teu sin leu
Pardon?	Xin nhắc lại?	sin njac lai
I like/do not like it.	Tôi rât/không thích.	teu ra´/chong tik`
May I take your photograph?	Tôi đủọc phep chup anh?	teu dög feb djub an

SYMBOLS

EATING & DRINKING

English	Vietnamese	Pronunciation
Please reserve us a table for four people for this evening.	ông/bà làm o 'n, cho chúng tôi một bàn bốn ngươ 'i tối nay.	ong/bah lahm ön, tscho tschung teu mot´ bahn bohn n´öi teunai
The menu, please.	Làm o'n cho tôi thưc đo 'n	lahm ön tscho teu tuk dön
salt/pepper/sugar	muối/tiêu/đừờng	meu/tiu/döng
cold/salty/undercooked	lanh/mặn/chưa chín	lann/mang/djua djin
with/without ice	có đá/không có đá	go da/chong go da
sparkling/still	có gas/không có gas	go gas/chong go gas
(no) drinking water	(không) nước uống	(chong) nök ung
vegetarian/allergy	ngườì ăn chay/dị ứng	n´öi an djai/di üng
Can we pay, please?	Làm o 'n tính tiền?	lahm ön, tön dien
cash/debit card/credit card	tiền mặt/thẻ tín dụng/ thẻ tín dụng	dien ma`/te tön sjung/ te tön sjung

MISCELLANEOUS

English	Vietnamese	Pronunciation
Where is …?	ở đâu có …?	ö dau go
What time is it?	Mây giờ rôi?	mai sjö reu
today/tomorrow/ yesterday	hôm này/ngáy may/ hôm qua	hom nai/nai mai/hom hoa
How much is it?	Gía bao nhiêu?	ja bau nju
I would like to rent …	Tôi muôn thuê …	teu mu-en tü-e
a car/a bicycle	ô-tô/xe đạp	otoh/säa dab
Where is there internet access/WiFi?	Nôi truy câp internet/ sóng?	neu dschi gap internet/song
pharmacy	nhà thuốc tây	nja tuok dai
fever/ache	sốt/đau	sot`/dau
diarrhoea/sickness	tiêu chảy/ói mử	diu djai/eu mua
forbidden/dangerous	câm/nguy hiêm	gam/nji hem
left/right	trái/phải	dschei/fei
expensive/cheap	đắt/re'	dak/rea
0/1/2/3/4/5/6/7/8/9/10/ 100/1000	khong/một/hai/ba/bốn/ năm/sáu/bảy/tám/ chin'/mười/một trăm/ một ngàn	chong/mot´/hai/bah/ bohn/nam/sau/bei/ dahm/tschin/muö/ modscham/modnjahn

HOLIDAY VIBES

FOR RELAXATION & CHILLING

FOR BOOKWORMS & FILM BUFFS

 MASTER HU'S BLACK POWDER
A crime novel (2010) from the Tran Nhut sisters: Mandarin Tan must solve ghostly mysteries – an exciting journey into the 17th century.

 **THE SCENT OF GREEN PAPAYA**
Feature film by Vietnamese-French director Tran Anh Hung about ten years of the life of a girl called Mui, who moved to Saigon from a village when she was 12 to work as a servant (1993).

BE FREE, WHOEVER YOU ARE
Thich Nhat Hanh is a best-selling author among monks who write. His works include this small book full of wisdom, on happiness, (inner) freedom and human dignity (2015).

 APOCALYPSE NOW
Get goosebumps with the unforgettable scene of helicopters flying to the accompaniment of "The Ride of the Valkyries" and Marlon Brando as the crazed Colonel Kurtz in Francis Ford Coppola's Oscar-winning masterpiece about the Vietnam War (1979).

PLAYLIST ON SHUFFLE

❚❚ **BIG DADDY** – NOI VOI EM
Great, melodic rap. This young man has star quality!

► **SUBOI** – CONG
The queen of electro hip hop: Vietnam's first female rapper sounds as if she's come straight from the Bronx

► **THANH LAM** – NOI BINH YEN
One of Vietnam's most popular female singers, with a powerful romantic voice

► **HUONG THANH** – DRAGONFLY
The finest melancholy Vietnamese world music

► **NGUYEN LE** – CELEBRATING THE DARK SIDE OF THE MOON
The jazz guitarist is a true master of the strings and is celebrated in other parts of the world

► **BINH MINH VU** – MOI TINH DAU
Songs about heartbreak actually made in Germany, but sounding as if they are straight out of Vietnam

Your holiday soundtrack can be found on **Spotify** *under* **MARCO POLO Vietnam**

Or scan this code with the Spotify app
● ·|||||||||||·|··||||·

ONLINE

BUSMAP.VN
The free English-language app helps tourists navigate the jungle of around 100 bus lines in Ho Chi Minh City and Hanoi

HANOI GRAPEVINE
This account on X (formerly Twitter) gives you an overview of the young art and culture scene in Vietnam. *(x.com/HanoiGrapevine)*

VIETNAMESE RECIPES
Yum – this free app provides recipes to try when you get home!

FOODY
This free app provides insider tips from Vietnamese locals, so you can find the nearest great soup restaurant. More and more reviews are being posted in English

GRAB
The Vietnamese version of Uber is safe and comfortable, but here you have the option to pay the taxi or moped taxi in cash or by card (not available across the entire country)

TRAVEL PURSUIT

THE MARCO POLO HOLIDAY QUIZ

Do you know what makes Vietnam tick? Test your knowledge of the idiosyncrasies and eccentricities of the country and its people. The answers are at the foot of the page, with further details on pages 18 to 23.

❶ How are the figures moved at water puppet theatres?
a) With red-gold strings
b) With rods
c) With hands in velvet gloves

❷ Who do the Vietnamese turn to if they need advice from their ancestors?
a) Uncle Ho
b) The abbot in the district's pagoda
c) A fortune teller or shaman

❸ What are the walking streets in the major cities for?
a) An evening stroll at the weekend
b) Walking meditation
c) To keep fit by doing Nordic walking early in the morning

❹ What culinary speciality is found particularly in the north?
a) Grilled mouse brains
b) Red raspberries on skewers
c) Dog meat

❺ Which religion did the early Cham bring to Vietnam?
a) Christianity
b) Hinduism
c) Buddhism

❻ How much of Vietnam is still covered by tropical forest?
a) 29 per cent
b) 12 per cent
c) 5 per cent

Vietnam's number one food: rice terraces in Mu Cang Chai

❼ What is typical Vietnamese "copy art"?
a) Famous paintings, which are copied again and again from generation to generation
b) Excellent, surprising modern printing techniques, created on copying machines
c) A "real" picture by Picasso for an incredible £50

❽ Why do the Vietnamese like to ask people their age?
a) Because of the Confucian social order
b) To work out how high they can start negotiating a price
c) Out of pure interest

❾ What does the god Shiva ride on in Cham culture?
a) An elephant
b) A bull
c) A dragon

❿ What did Ho Chi Minh want to happen to his ashes after he died?
a) He wanted them put in a golden urn in the mausoleum in Hanoi
b) He wanted them scattered in Hanoi
c) He wanted them to be divided into three urns

⓫ What religious group has been present in Vietnam since 1926?
a) The Cao Dai sect
b) The Quan Am sect
c) The Ngoc Hoang sect

⓬ How many rice harvests can there be each year in the Mekong Delta?
a) Only one
b) Up to three
c) Five to ten, depending on the rains

INDEX

WE WANT TO HEAR FROM YOU!

Did you have a great holiday? Is there something on your mind? Whatever it is, let us know! Whether you want to praise the guide, alert us to errors or give us a personal tip – MARCO POLO would be pleased to hear from you.

Please contact us by email:
sales@heartwoodpublishing.co.uk

We do everything we can to provide the very latest information for your trip. Nevertheless, despite all of our authors' thorough research, errors can creep in. MARCO POLO does not accept any liability for this.

PICTURE CREDITS
Cover photo: Reisfeld bei Sa Pa (AWL Images: M. Matteo)
Photos: DuMont Bildarchiv: Krause (64, 115); huber-images: S. Bennett (24/25), T. Draper (49), Gräfenhain (57, 102, 120), R. Taylor (27); huber-images/Picture Finders (23); F. Ihlow (rear flap); Laif: M. Sasse (99, 105, 117); mauritius images: Kugler (81); mauritius images/age (59); mauritius images/Alamy (54/55, 74, 87, 88), A. Bain (32/33), H. Hanh Mac Thi (26/27), Quang Nguyen Vinh (110), P. Raja Kannaiah (132/133), S. Reboredo (2/3), I. Vdovin (front outer flap, front inner flap, 1); mauritius images/Alamy/Asia (61, 67), Duy Phuong Nguyen (73); mauritius images/Alamy/China Span: K. Su (142/143, 144/145); mauritius images/Alamy/RosaIreneBetancourt 14 (31); mauritius images/Alamy/Zoonar GmbH (19); mauritius images/Image Source: S. Barr (10); mauritius images/imagebroker: B. Bieder (124/125); mauritius images/Imagebroker: J. Hiltmann (47); mauritius images/robertharding (68/69); M. Miethig (147); T. Stankie-wicz (9, 83); M. Weigt (6/7, 8, 11, 12/13, 14/15, 20, 30/31, 34/35, 38/39, 44, 50, 53, 62, 76, 91, 92, 94/95, 107, 112, 118, 122, 135); White Star: Schiefer (109)

4th Edition – fully revised and updated 2024
Worldwide Distribution: Heartwood Publishing Ltd, Bath, United Kingdom
www.heartwoodpublishing.co.uk

Authors: Martina Miethig
Editor: Franziska Kahl
Picture editor: Gabriele Forst
Cartography: © MAIRDUMONT, Ostfildern (pp. 36–37, 126, 128, 130, inner jacket, outer jacket, folding map); © MAIRDUMONT, Ostfildern, use of map data from OpenStreetMap, Lizenz CC-BY-SA 2.0 (pp. 40–41, 43, 70–71, 79, 85, 96–97, 100)
Cover design and pull-out map cover design: bilekjaeger_Kreativagentur with Zukunftswerkstatt, Stuttgart
Page design: Langenstein Communication GmbH, Ludwigsburg

Heartwood Publishing credits:
Translated from the German by Thomas Moser, Mo Croasdale
Editors: Rosamund Sales, Kate Michell
Prepress: Summerlane Books, Bath
Printed in India

MARCO POLO AUTHOR
MARTINA MIETHIG

She has cursed the country many times, for example, when her glasses were stolen from the end of her nose when she was on a *cyclo* in Ho Chi Minh City, or when there was a bat sitting in the toilet that she went to in Hue. But Martina has come to love Vietnam and its people. She has been visiting the country since 1994, and has written guidebooks and coffee table books, and reported on it for radio and magazines *(GeckoStories.com)*.

DOS & DON'TS

HOW TO AVOID SLIP-UPS AND BLUNDERS

DON'T TRAVEL DURING THE TET FESTIVAL

At Tet, the Vietnamese New Year, the whole of Vietnam is on the move. Tours and tickets sell out quickly and are extremely expensive. Public services shut down for a week, and many restaurants and shops close too.

DON'T GIVE MONEY TO BEGGARS

It's normal to feel compassion for people, but bear in mind that there are thousands of professional beggars in Vietnam, who are being exploited by ruthless criminals. Donate your money to a relief organisation instead (see p. 137).

DON'T PAY TOO MUCH

When paying for a taxi or *cyclo*, at the ticket counter for the Citadel in Hue, or buying fruit on the street, make a note of the value of the banknote you hand over – otherwise you risk the rather common problem that the seller will claim to have received a 10,000 dong note instead of a 100,000 dong note. And be just as careful checking the change that you get back!

DON'T TOUCH THE MONKS

Buddhist monks are not allowed to be touched by women. If you would like to present a gift to a monk, do so through someone else, such as a tour guide. Also, wait to be offered a hand to shake – if a monk doesn't offer you his hand, do not under any circumstances take the initiative.

DON'T VISIT NATIONAL PARKS AT THE WEEKEND

You can't expect to hear nothing but the birds in the national parks at weekends because the trails and the accommodation are often overrun with troops of Vietnamese, with lots of beer and loud music.